THE PILGRIMAGE WAY
OF THE CROSS

THE PILGRIMAGE
WAY OF THE CROSS

EDWARD HAYS

FOREST OF PEACE
Publishing

Suppliers for the Spiritual Pilgrim
Leavenworth, KS

Other Books by the Author:
(available through Forest of Peace Publishing or your favorite bookstore)

Prayers and Rituals

Psalms for Zero Gravity
Prayers for a Planetary Pilgrim
Prayers for the Domestic Church
Prayers for the Servants of God

Parables and Stories

Little Orphan Angela
The Gospel of Gabriel
The Quest for the Flaming Pearl
St. George and the Dragon
The Magic Lantern
The Ethiopian Tattoo Shop
Twelve and One-Half Keys
Sundancer
The Christmas Eve Storyteller

Contemporary Spirituality

Prayer Notes to a Friend
The Great Escape Manual
The Ladder
The Old Hermit's Almanac
The Lenten Labyrinth
A Lenten Hobo Honeymoon
Holy Fools & Mad Hatters
A Pilgrim's Almanac
Pray All Ways
Secular Sanctity
In Pursuit of the Great White Rabbit
The Ascent of the Mountain of God
Feathers on the Wind

THE PILGRIMAGE WAY OF THE CROSS

copyright © 2003, by Edward M. Hays

Library of Congress Cataloging-in-Publication Data

Hays, Edward M.
  The pilgrimage Way of the Cross / Edward Hays.
    p. cm.
  ISBN 0-939516-68-3 (alk. paper)
  1. Lent—Prayer-books and devotions—English. 2. Stations of the Cross. I. Title.
  BV85.H466 2003
  242'.34—dc21

                          2002152192

published by
Forest of Peace Publishing, Inc.
PO Box 269
Leavenworth, KS 66048-0269 USA
1-800-659-3227
www.forestofpeace.com

printed by
Hall Commercial Printing
Topeka, KS 66608-0007

1st printing: January 2003

Illustrations by Edward Hays
The photos on pages 144, 180 and 214 are used with permission of www.BiblePlaces.com
The photos on pages 92 and 175 are from the Model at the Holy Land Hotel in Jerusalem

DEDICATION

TO

*Murray and Mary Rogers
and Heather Sanderman,
the Jyotiniketan Community*

"The challenge to us Christians today is whether through
our faith and life in the Resurrected Christ we will be
able to transform the powers of hatred, destruction and
death into a potential of love and peace."

–Father Murray Rogers,
in a note written in Jerusalem in 1974

HISTORICAL NOTE

While on a personal pilgrimage to Jerusalem in 1971, the author
had the privilege to meet and be hosted by three members of
the small Anglican ecumenical community of Jyotiniketan, then
located in the Old City. In 1974, Thomas Turkle, my publisher,
was their guest on his pilgrimage to the Holy City. And ten
years after my sojourn, Thomas Skorupa, my editor, made a
pilgrimage to Jerusalem and was also graciously hosted by the
community. The three of us dedicate this book to these three
remarkable and holy people.

The Old City of Jerusalem as Viewed from the Mount of Olives

TABLE OF CONTENTS

A NOTE ON THE ART IN THIS BOOK

The logo used to mark each of these Stations of the Cross is a cross rising up out of the turbulent and fertile waters of baptism, the overriding theme of this Pilgrimage Way of the Cross.

Other than the drawings of the Jordan River (*page 25*) and St. George's Monastery (*page 42*), the pencil art images in this book are not illustrations but are intended as meditational images. When you come upon one of these "Visual Reflections," you are encouraged to pause and reflect upon it for a few moments, an act that will require some discipline. While we are quite capable of reading and understanding the printed word, our ability to read the messages in symbolic imagery is becoming a lost art. We live in an image-inundated world, in a blizzard of billions of brilliant images flashing out from television, movies, computers and endless advertisements. The consequence of this pictorial deluge is a deadening of our capacity to see symbolically. Words speak to the mind, but symbols speak to the soul. May your passage through this book help you to progress beyond the habit of merely looking and to engage in the ancient art of seeing and reading the symbolic messages in art.

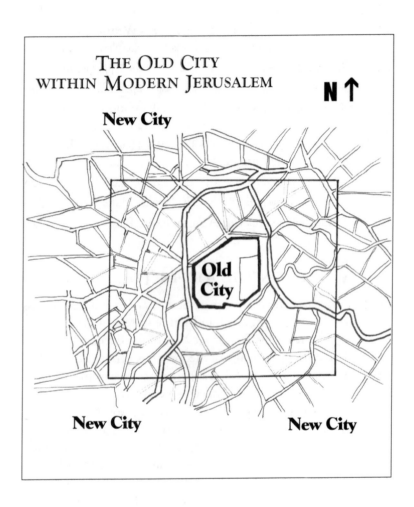

THE OLD CITY
WITHIN MODERN JERUSALEM

N ↑

New City

Old
City

New City

New City

The geographical pilgrimage is the symbolic acting out of an interior journey.

—Thomas Merton, *Mystics and Zen Masters*

Jerusalem is a small town of big things; and the average modern city is a big town full of small things. All the most important and interesting powers in history are here gathered within the area of a quiet village; and if they are not always friends, at least they are necessarily neighbors.

—Gilbert K. Chesterton, *The New Jerusalem*

The road to the sacred leads through the secular.

—Abraham Heschel

Jerusalem, my happy home,
When shall I come to thee?
When shall my sorrows have an end,
Thy joys when shall I see?

—Old English Song

The Western Wall and the Dome of the Rock within the Old City

PREFACE

In 1971 I had the privilege of spending two months as a pilgrim in the Holy Land, the majority of the time in the Old City of Jerusalem. Because my living quarters were in the Muslim Quarter along the Via Dolorosa, I had easy access to the Christian shrines and holy places of the Old City. While I also spent time in Galilee and visited Jericho and the area around the Dead Sea, it was my weeks in the venerable ancient city that captured my heart and my soul. Along with visiting various Christian shrines, by using a Jewish prayer shawl, I was able to pray at the Western Wall. I also made a prayerful visit to the Mosque of the Dome of the Rock and recited psalms as I walked along the walls of the Old City. In writing this *Pilgrimage Way of the Cross*, I was transported back to the stunning sights, the sensuous smells and the many other vivid impressions of my personal pilgrimage to Jerusalem. It is my hope that this small book, which hardly touches upon all of its sacred places, will enable you the reader to experience being a pilgrim to the Holy City.

A NOTE
regarding the names in the maps and directions in this book

The streets, roads and many sites in the Holy Land have changed names since I visited there, and they continue to change names even as this book is being written. While every attempt has been made to provide geographical accuracy, the intention of the author was not to write a tourist guidebook but rather to give the reader a lived experience of being a pilgrim in the Holy City.

A Station of the Cross Along the Via Dolorosa

A Brief History of the Stations

Found in both the Eastern Orthodox and Western Roman Churches, the Stations of the Cross is a popular devotion honoring the passion and death of Jesus Christ. This religious practice has its origins in Holy Land pilgrimages to the route Christ used in carrying his cross to his death on Calvary and the burial site nearby. The earliest pilgrims would walk the Way of the Cross without established places to stop and prayerfully meditate on a particular aspect of Christ's passion. Some of these early cross processions began on the Mount of Olives at the Garden of Gethsemane where Jesus was arrested and would then enter the Holy City by St. Stephen's Gate along what was known as the *Via Dolorosa*, the Way of Sorrows.

The twelfth century saw a surge of popular devotion centering on the passion and death of Jesus. However, medieval pilgrimages were severely restricted because of the endless warfare of the Crusades after the Muslims captured Jerusalem. St. Francis of Assisi is credited with creating a substitute pilgrimage by which the homebound faithful could experience a bodily prayer reflection on the passion. This expanded into pilgrimages to a series of station churches located across the countryside that commemorated particular sites of Christ's passion.

In 1343 the Franciscan Friars who had been given custody of all the Holy Land shrines established the tradition of the fourteen stations along the Via Dolorosa. By the seventeenth and eighteenth centuries, fixing the number of stations at fourteen had become the general norm worldwide. Modern pilgrims to Jerusalem still commonly walk the Franciscan Way.

The next development in this devotion was erecting inside an individual church all fourteen shrines that once had been housed in fourteen separate churches. Along the side walls of a church were placed fourteen plaques bearing art images of the various events of Christ's passion. Christians made personal or communal parish pilgrimages inside the church building by walking from station to station, praying and reflecting at each one. The traditional devotional prayers of the Way of the Cross that are used by most parishes were created by the Redemptorist priest St. Alphonsus Liguori, who lived from 1696 to 1787. He based his prayers on the original fourteen stations devised by the Holy Land Francsicans.

While the season of Lent has become the customary time for communal celebrations of the Stations of the Cross, as private devotions they have been prayed at any time during the year.

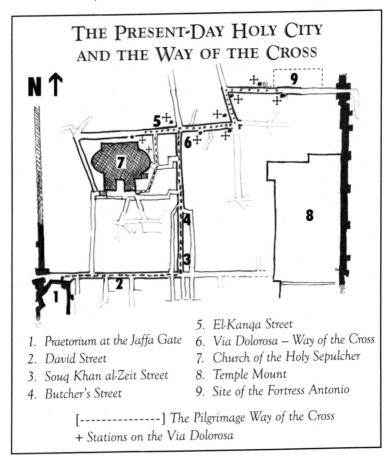

THE PRESENT-DAY HOLY CITY AND THE WAY OF THE CROSS

1. Praetorium at the Jaffa Gate
2. David Street
3. Souq Khan al-Zeit Street
4. Butcher's Street
5. El-Kanqa Street
6. Via Dolorosa – Way of the Cross
7. Church of the Holy Sepulcher
8. Temple Mount
9. Site of the Fortress Antonio

[---------------] The Pilgrimage Way of the Cross
+ Stations on the Via Dolorosa

THE NEW TWENTY STATIONS OF THE CROSS

At the end of the twentieth century a new version of the Stations of the Cross arose. It was based on the events of the passion as recorded in the gospels, and also included the resurrection of Christ. In 1991 in the ancient Roman Coliseum, Pope John Paul II began to lead the crowds in these new Stations.

The twenty stations in this book include some ancient pilgrimage sites not found among the original fourteen stations or in the version inspired by the Vatican II liturgical renewal. While, like the traditional Stations, they can be prayed any time, *The Pilgrimage Way of the Cross* was additionally created as a daily Lenten handbook. It divides the forty days of Lent among the twenty stations visited in these pages. There is a reflection for each day of Lent, as well as the major feasts of the Easter season, to encourage your further reflection at the various stations. Spending two or more days at some stations will help you deepen your experience at these significant sites along the Way of the Cross.

It is hoped that these new Stations of the Cross will provide a real pilgrimage experience for homebound and workbound pilgrims. Many of us desire someday to go on pilgrimage to the Holy Land, but as in medieval times the dangers of travel to the Near East, as well as the cost and personal family responsibilities, make such a trip prohibitive for the majority of Christians. If you are fortunate enough to have actually made a pilgrimage to the Holy Land, may these stations be a prayerful remembrance and a revival of that religious experience.

While pilgrims pray with their feet, *The Pilgrimage Way of the Cross* is not so much a geographic as a soul pilgrimage to the Holy City of three great religions — Judaism, Christianity and Islam. This is a sacred journey intended for those who carry their personal crosses as they follow prayerfully behind their beloved cross-burdened Savior. Yet the route you will travel

Jesus Embracing His Cross

is not only the *Via Dolorosa*, the Way of the Sorrows, but also the *Via Gaudioso*, the Way of Joy, since this path ends in the victorious joy of the Resurrection, Ascension and Coming of the Holy Spirit.

If you begin this pilgrimage of the soul on the eve of Ash Wednesday, you will find that each Sunday is a day of rest for prayer and reflection. Such "rest days" and "extra days" are typically part of an organized pilgrimage group. This book's reflections for Lenten Sundays allow you to visit a shrine in the area of the previous station, a holy place that may or may not be directly related to the Way of the Cross. Walk this pilgrimage at your own pace, perhaps spending several days at some stations, reflecting and praying over the significance of the site.

The prayer of each day begins with the invitational, "We praise you and we follow, O Christ, because by our crosses united we redeem the world." The pronoun used is in the plural, for following Christ and sharing in the redemption of the world is a corporate act. Each day concludes with the personal prayer petition, "Let me take up my cross and follow you, Lord Jesus, for by so doing I share in the liberation of the world." The pronoun in this prayer is personal to remind you of the importance of your individual active involvement in this saving action. Consider reciting these prayers and the Scripture of the day in a soft audible voice, for the more senses you involve in praying, the more and the better you will pray.

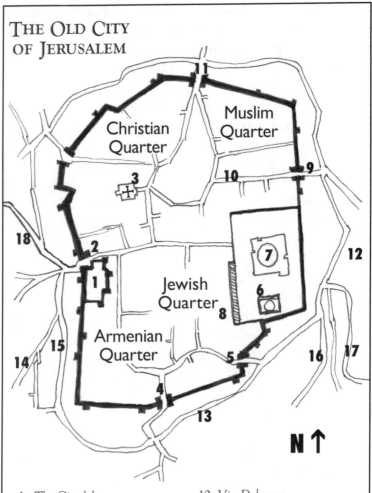

THE OLD CITY OF JERUSALEM

Christian Quarter

Muslim Quarter

Jewish Quarter

Armenian Quarter

N ↑

1. The Citadel
2. Jaffa (David's) Gate
3. Church of the Holy Sepulcher
4. Zion Gate
5. Dung Gate
6. Temple Mount
7. Dome of the Rock
8. Western Wall
9. St. Stephen's Gate

10. Via Dolorosa
11. Damascus Gate
12. The Mount of Olives
13. Maale Ha-Shalom Road
14. Hativat Yerushalayim Road
15. Khajivat Etsyoni Road
16. Derekh Ha-Ofel Road
17. Derekh Yerikho-Jericho Road
18. Jaffa Road

THE HOLY CITY

I rejoiced when they said to me,
"Let us go to God's house."
And now our feet are standing
within your gates, O Jerusalem.
Jerusalem built as a city
walled round about....
May peace be within your ramparts,
prosperity within your towers....

—Psalm 122: 1-3, 7

As a pilgrim to the Holy Land, after landing at Tel Aviv's airport, you travel to Jerusalem, arriving at what is known as the Jaffa Gate, which is located on the west wall of the Old City. It derives its name from the fact that it was the end of the road when traveling to Jerusalem from the old seaport city of Jaffa. Also known as David's Gate, after King David, for centuries it has been the traditional entrance gate for pilgrims to the Holy City.

As you gaze on the gray stone walls of the Old City, so named since it is now surrounded by the modern city of Jerusalem (*see map on page 10*), pause and remember that this is a Holy City to the three great western religions. It is divided into four quarters: the Armenian quarter, the Jewish quarter, the Christian quarter and the Muslim quarter. Contained within these old walls are centuries of religious history and holy shrines saturated with sacred memories for Jews, Christians and Muslims. Since God cannot be the exclusive property of one people, this Holy City does not belong to anyone — it belongs to everyone. While her ancient streets are soaked red with centuries of blood and echo with hate-filled violence, she continues to hold a mystical

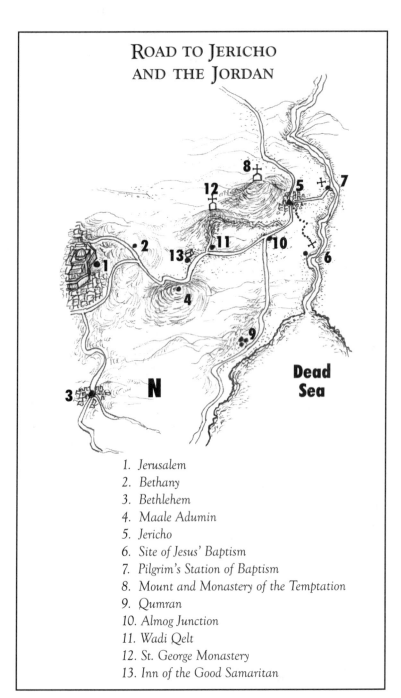

ROAD TO JERICHO AND THE JORDAN

Dead Sea

N

1. Jerusalem
2. Bethany
3. Bethlehem
4. Maale Adumin
5. Jericho
6. Site of Jesus' Baptism
7. Pilgrim's Station of Baptism
8. Mount and Monastery of the Temptation
9. Qumran
10. Almog Junction
11. Wadi Qelt
12. St. George Monastery
13. Inn of the Good Samaritan

attraction for pilgrims of each of the three religions and for visitors who have no religion. The crowded, narrow, alley-like streets and the aged buildings mark this sacred city's ancient character. This seemingly endlessly bleeding, suffering city of antiquity named Salem — "Peace" — is like a priceless jewel set in the center of the surrounding ring of the modern, bustling city of Jerusalem.

Unlike the path followed by centuries of pilgrims, our Pilgrimage Way of the Cross does not begin by entering the Holy City through David's Gate. Instead, we turn to our right from this arched gateway and begin our journey down the *Khajivat Etsyoni* Road (*see map on page 20*), which runs parallel to the *Hativat Yerushalayim*, walking to the site of our first station, the Jordan River outside of Jericho, where Jesus was baptized.

The Jericho Road

This road winds its way eastward along the southern walls of the Mount Zion section of Jerusalem in order to connect with the road to Jericho at the Mount of Olives. On the left is an area known to Muslims as *Haram Esh-Sharif*, the Noble Sanctuary, and to Jews as *Har Ha-Bayit*, the Temple Mount. Once, the entire Temple Mount covered more than thirty-five acres, which is approximately the size of thirty-four football fields placed side by side. At the time of Jesus the great religious festivals in this massive temple area would often have been crowded with hundreds of thousands of pilgrims along with innumerable sacrificial animals.

The massive artificial stone mound was built on what was believed to be the Mountain of Moriah, the traditional site where the Patriarch Abraham came to sacrifice his son Isaac. It was here that King Solomon built the first Israelite Temple. When the Babylonians destroyed that first great temple, King Herod constructed his magnificent temple on the very same mount, and it was to this temple that Jesus of Galilee came on pilgrimage. Now standing on this holy site is the holy Mosque of the Rock with its beautiful golden dome, the most recognized symbol of Jerusalem. After those at Mecca and Medina, it is Islam's most hallowed shrine. Today all that remains of the once majestic temple of King Herod is found on the west side of the Mount, the towering massive stone Western, or Wailing, Wall, which is a most sacred site for the Jewish people. (See the Political Postlogue, page 239, for the historical implications of Mount Moriah, and the Appendix for more on Muhammad and the Dome of the Rock Mosque.)

Having reached the Jericho Road, we turn right and proceed up and over the Mount of Olives to Bethany, the village of Jesus' friends Martha and Mary. After cresting the Mount of Olives, the road weaves its way 23 miles down through the barren wilderness toward Jericho. In this brief stretch not only does the scenery radically change — from the lush green of the Mount of Olives to the brownish tones of the barren desert — so does the temperature. The thermometer drastically rises as we descend from 2250 feet above sea level to 900 feet below sea level! As this Jericho road twists and turns in its descent eastward, it is devoid of life except for an occasional Bedouin camp of black tents.

With your imagination, allow your feet to pray as you realize that you are walking in the footsteps of countless pilgrims. Hidden in the dust of this road are the footprints of a certain carpenter-craftsman named Jesus of Nazareth, who long ago came this very way on a holy journey to the Jordan River. As we proceed on the road, without warning, out of the waves of heat rising up from the desert, like a hazy mirage there appears a lush green oasis of trees surrounding the ancient city of Jericho, whose walls came tumbling down at the blaring horns of Joshua. It is one of history's oldest inhabited places; archeological excavations reveal that it was a walled city dating back to at least 6800 B.C.

The traditional location of the baptism of Jesus at the Jordan today, sadly, is a restricted Israeli military zone. Christian pilgrims are allowed at that site only once a year on the third Thursday in October. Our pilgrimage destination is east of Jericho, so we bypass the city and proceed toward this alternate site of Jesus' baptism (see #7 in map on page 22). The surrounding area is impressive not for any natural beauty but because of its strikingly austere desert barrenness. The Jordan flows south out of Galilee into the Jordan valley. Here it is about 90 feet wide and only 3 to 10 feet deep — its banks covered with dense thickets of willows and underbrush.

THE JORDAN RIVER

Reflection

The actual site of the baptism of Jesus is less important than the significance of the act. Didn't his plunge into the Jordan make the whole river holy and all water sacred? Holy was the water with which you were — or will be — baptized, regardless of the river or spring from which it came. You are fortunate if you were baptized as an adult, for then you can visualize the site and the persons who shared that joyful occasion with you and witnessed your desire to live a new and dynamic kind of life.

If you were baptized as an infant, let these waters of the Jordan remind you how your parents and godparents had you plunged into the cross, death and resurrection of Christ. At some point later in your life you made a post-baptismal decision to live out that significant infant event, or you would not be making this pilgrimage. Let this Station of the Cross at the Jordan cause you to rededicate yourself with gratitude to the lifelong implications of being plunged into the dying and rising of Jesus Christ.

Make an act of dedication now, striving to allow the graces of your baptism to surface so you will become a faithful, loving and prayerful disciple of Christ.

+

Let me take up my cross and follow you, Lord Jesus,
for by so doing I share in the liberation of the world.

Ash Wednesday

THE FIRST STATION

THE BAPTISM OF JESUS IN THE JORDAN

*We praise you and we follow you, O Christ,
because by our crosses united, we redeem the world.*

Scripture for the First Station

*John the Baptist appeared in the desert proclaiming a baptism of
repentance for the forgiveness of sins...(and) it happened in those days
that Jesus came from Nazareth of Galilee and was baptized by John
in the Jordan. On coming up out of the water he saw the heavens
being torn open and the Spirit, like a dove, descending upon him. And
a voice came from the heavens, "You are my beloved Son; upon you
my favor rests." —*Mark 1: 4-5, 9-11

Did John the Baptist or anyone else in that crowd along the

JESUS IS GIVEN THE HOLY SPIRIT AS WELL AS HIS CROSS

Jordan's banks hear in the last fading echoes of the Voice that rumbled from the clouds, "and also, Jesus my beloved, upon you a *cross* shall rest"? The baptism of Jesus involved his investment in living as fully as possible as God's beloved son — including the consequences of the cross. For Jesus of Nazareth, the ignominious end of life on the Mount of Skulls outside Jerusalem began with his birth into a new life in the watery womb of the Jordan. From the moment Jesus rose up from his baptism, he knew he had to embrace the burden-cross that came with being a living mirror of God's love, pardon and compassion. God never gives a cross that totally crushes, that is ultimately unbearable. So, besides the cross of God's favor and sonship that weighed upon Jesus' soul, there rested God's Spirit, empowering him to be the image of God's forgiveness and tender mercy.

Baptismal Cross Prayer

Risen Jesus, your death and resurrection
    were foreshadowed by your willing descent
    into Jordan's tomb-waters and your rising
    to a new life infused by the Holy Spirit.
Grace my eyes to look upon my baptism
    as a revelation of my own death and resurrection.
Empowered by the Holy Spirit, you embraced with love
    the cross-edged responsibility of being
    a daily mirror of God's love, mercy and power.
May I likewise be Spirit-touched
    so I may take up my baptismal cross and daily become
    a living mirror of God's love and compassion.

+

Let me take up my cross and follow you, Lord Jesus,
for by so doing I share in the liberation of the world.

The Second Day of the Pilgrimage
Ash Thursday

Cosmic Water

We praise you and we follow you, O Christ,
because by our crosses united, we redeem the world.

Scripture for the Second Day
"This is how all will know that you are my disciples...." — John 13: 35

Christians, it seems, suffer from Baptism Amnesia. We seem to easily forget how our very nature was radically transformed by that watery initiation, and so we appear no different in our actions or speech. Baptism makes us disciples of Jesus, and he supposed that his disciples would be easily recognized by their behavior. As he told Philip, those who had seen him had seen — had experienced — the Father. The same was to be true for his followers in every age. Sadly, instead of a Godlike response to life's daily incidents, so often ours is merely a human reaction.

The majority of Christians, being baptized as infants, have never made the proper baptismal journey. The journey of adult candidates preparing for baptism has three stages, echoing the process of our pilgrimage of the cross. The first stage is the departure from one's former life, symbolized by our traveling a road that leads away from the busy political and social life of the city of Jerusalem. The second stage was reflected in the 23 miles of desolate no-man's desert that we traveled to reach the Jordan, representing the in-between stage of being no longer part of the old and not yet part of the new. The third stage is the re-entry into one's former life but as a radically new person. We will experience this phase as we return to the world — to all the bustle, business and busyness of Jerusalem.

The primary theme of the Lenten song is renunciation, for that is the first act of anyone seeking baptism and abundant new life. To live out your baptism means rejecting your culture's way of responding to life and, instead, embracing God's way. This renunciation is not a rejection of the joys and beauties of the world but, rather, of the unredeemed ways of the world: violence, ruthless exploitation, division, greed, lust, war, aggression....

The water into which Jesus was plunged symbolized the primal cosmic element of creation out of which all life arose.

The Dead Sea

He and you were baptized into matter, the tangible stuff of the world that God originally created and blessed. Your baptism was a communion with God the water-maker, with all the raw material of the world, with all creatures and all created matter. The Risen Christ was intimately infused with all creation, revealing it in its original state as a wondrous divine gift. Jesus in his post-baptismal years proclaimed the world as God's gift to us and, most importantly, as our means of communion with the Divine Mystery.

Prayer at the Jordan

O God, grant me the grace
    to handle with reverence and wonder
    all I touch in this God-saturated world in which I live.
May my work and play, my leisure and loves
    be sacraments of communion with you.
Invest me with the courage and conviction
    to respond generously as a baptized disciple of Christ
    to all those I will encounter this day.
May my behavior and speech clearly identify me
    as your beloved.

+

Let me take up my cross and follow you, Lord Jesus,
for by so doing I share in the liberation of the world.

The Third Day of the Pilgrimage
Ash Friday

Meditation on the Baptism of Jesus in the Jordan

We praise you and we follow you, O Christ,
because by our crosses united, we redeem the world.

Scripture for the Third Day

"*Whoever wishes to come after me must deny himself, take up his cross and follow me.*" —Mark 8: 34

We linger a second day after the First Station here on the shore of the Jordan River where the Prophet John baptized Jesus of Nazareth. Here along the banks of this holy river of the Promised Land, among the thickets of slender green willows bowing beneath the dry desert wind, one can sense the abiding presence of Jesus the Convert. We might think this title sits uneasily upon him; nevertheless, it does fit him well, for he truly experienced a life conversion. As we reflect, a prayer surfaces:

As Prophet John plunged Jesus in this shallow river
    into the bath of his mission and his cross,
    you, O God, spoke from an overhanging cloud to his heart,
    calling him to leave his lifelong work as a village carpenter
    to become a wandering singer of your good news.
As a dripping-wet Jesus arose out of the Jordan's swirling waters,
    you placed upon his shoulders an invisible cross.
I desire that the cross placed upon me during this pilgrimage
    be no temporary sign,
    like the blackened ashes of Ash Wednesday.

I yearn that an unwashable, permanent cross
　　be daily imprinted upon me,
　　marking me as a true disciple of Christ the Cross Carrier.
Indeed, I'm reluctant to carry a cross,
　　so I pray that the waters of the Jordon that surge past me
　　carry away within their current all my apprehensions and fears
　　at bearing the burden of my cross.
O God, Giver all gifts,
　　as you laid an invisible cross upon Jesus' shoulders,
　　grant me the same gift.

Even if you give me a too-visible cross of some physical affliction,
　　may I open my arms to it with gratitude.
Make me conscious that by my baptism
　　I have become a convert of the cross,
　　since I was baptized into the cross, death and resurrection
　　of my Lord.
Jesus told us that the primary requirement
　　for all those wishing to walk with him
　　was to take up their crosses and follow him.
I confess, O God, that I fear pain,
　　and I shun the suffering of any kind of cross.
So grant me the courage
　　to clutch with passionate love my unique and personal cross

as the instrument of my salvation and that of the entire world.
O Divine One, you know my strengths and weaknesses,
and which crosses I am capable of carrying.
O Holy Wisdom Spirit, enlighten me to know the difference
between my true cross and a painful burden
I myself have fashioned by my wrong life choices.
O God who never desires that your children suffer,
open my eyes so easily blinded by illusion
if I have identified as my cross some unfortunate situation
that neither you nor I wish me to embrace.

Take a moment now to pause in the Spirit's silence so you
may identify and name your unique redeeming cross or crosses.

Silent Reflection

Prayer of Accepting My Cross

*"Whoever does not take up his cross and follow after me is not worthy
of me."* —Matthew 10: 38

O divine and wise Giver of gifts,
I question whether I'm worthy of your love,
for so often I have rejected my cross.
I have judged it too heavy or too shameful,
gauging it a burden from which to escape.

By making this Pilgrimage of the Cross,
walking your Son's Way of the Cross,
may I learn how my cross has a secret purpose
in your sacred scheme of global redemption
so that I can embrace it as a love-gift from you.

+

*Let me take up my cross and follow you, Lord Jesus,
for by so doing I share in the liberation of the world.*

Visual Reflection

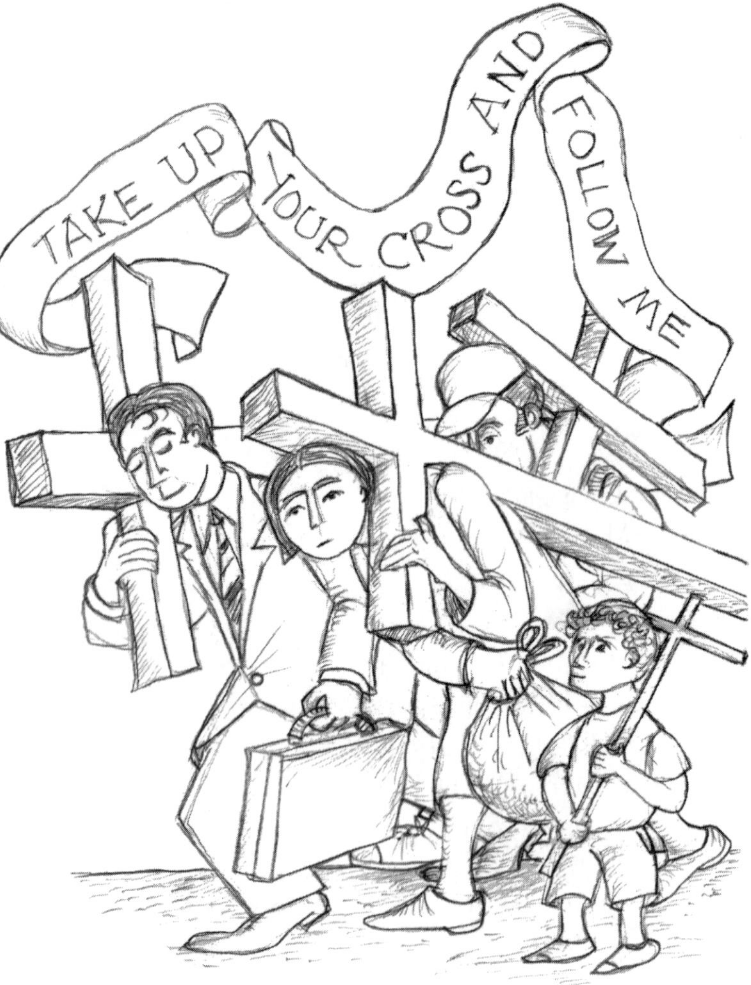

TAKE UP YOUR CROSS AND FOLLOW ME

In all of history no m ore unique requirement was ever given to become a disciple or the member of any group. For those wishing to join his company, Jesus never required high intelligence, a college or even high school education, any leadership or athletic abilities, any artistic or creative talents, or any previous discipleship experience. His requirement is embarrassingly simple – and, simultaneously, shockingly difficult: "If you wish to be my follower, you must take up your cross, deny your very self and follow me" (Mark 8: 34).

Moreover, Jesus fails to provide us with a catalog of Acceptable Crosses from which we are to choose our particular cross, or how to properly determine our crosses' correct size, shape or weight. He refrains from making all these possible requirements because he knows from his own flesh – in which the Divine Mystery was fully saturated – that he, and each one of us, was born with a cross!

At some times in our lives our cross seems absent, and we are often given a different cross at different stages of our lives. Still, Jesus never calls us to fashion a cross out of the stuff of our lives. We don't have to, for our cross is already there, always there, only waiting for us to embrace it as part of our life destiny. Since crosses are such embarrassing things to wear, they are often cleverly camouflaged by being given psychological, medical or sociological names – each of which has its own appropriate treatment or cure. There is, however, no cure for a cross!

We either embrace our cross or we curse it. We shoulder it or attempt to get rid of it. We try to hide it, or we receive it as our divinely given tool for growing to full maturity and into Godhood.

If, as a pilgrim on this road to Calvary, you feel that you've been slighted by not having been given a cross to carry, take a few moments to examine your life more carefully.

The Fourth Day of the Pilgrimage
Ash Saturday

The Desert Road of Temptation

We praise you and we follow you, O Christ,
because by our crosses united, we redeem the world.

Scripture for the Fourth Day

At once the Spirit drove him out into the desert, and he remained in the desert for forty days, tempted by Satan. He was among the wild beasts.... —Mark 1: 12-13

Leaving the banks of the Jordan, our pilgrimage journey now follows the path of Jesus away from this site. After his baptism he was led by the Spirit out into the desert to reflect in solitude on the implications of being called God's beloved son. Leaving behind the palm tree oasis of Jericho *(see map on page 22)*, if you look toward the west you will see a craggy, barren mountain jutting up against the horizon. The crusader pilgrims called it *Mont Quarantana*, "Mount of forty (days)." Today it is known as the Mount of the Temptation. Tradition maintains that in a cave high on this rocky mountain the Evil One tempted a praying Jesus. In his prayerful solitude it appears he became aware that he was to be the divine instrument for God's healing restoration of the world. Three times the Evil One tempted him to employ futile, self-defeating means to achieve this mission of liberating the world: to use regal authority, mystical powers, and domination instead of "weakness" and the cross.

At the top of this mountain is the small Greek Orthodox Monastery of the Temptation, clinging to the jagged cliffs like a wind-twisted scrub fir tree. In such a way did our tempted Lord cling to the good news he heard at his baptism; he clung to his belief that he was a beloved of God. Anchored by the roots of faith in that special identity, he held firmly to God's loving care for him, as the powerful Evil One tried to sway him to let go of his humanity by working wonders to prove he was the Chosen One of God. He resisted the enticement to achieve good by employing the ways of the world: power and prestige. While a beloved of God, he embraced the paradox that only in and through his vulnerable body, the weakness of his humanity, and not by working marvels and wonders, would God redeem the earth.

Although our pilgrimage does not include climbing to the monastery and its cave where Jesus wrestled with the Devil, by looking westward from the top of that mountain you can see in the distance the Mount of Olives, where the Evil One would again come to tempt a praying Jesus. Like the Master, you also frequently will be tempted to choose the ways of the world instead of the ways of your cross. Daily you will be tempted to be "practical" as you confront the realities of life. The seduction is to behave like a realistic son or daughter of the pragmatic world instead of responding as a beloved daughter or son of God. Pause at the foot of Mont Quarantana and pray for the gift of a clinging-roots belief in the reality that you, like Jesus, are a beloved of God. Pray to remember that upon you rest both the favor of God and the power of the Spirit. Strengthened by that baptismal belief, take up your cross today as we follow Jesus up to Jerusalem on the road west from Jericho and proceed northward through the barren wasteland to the green heights of the Mount of Olives.

Surely, after his deeply moving baptism experience, Jesus was visited by a "holy" temptation not to return to the world. After his solitude retreat he easily could have gone further into the desert instead of out of it. Was he perhaps tempted to become a member of the Essenes, a religious community whose monastery was located at *Qumran* on the northwest shore of the Dead Sea south of Jericho? The Essenes were a Jewish sect of men living a communal life separated from the world and the temple worship so as to live a pure life completely devoted to God. Jesus chose instead to return to the world — but not as the same person he was before his baptism. Traveling through the bleak desert wasteland on the same Jericho road, now transformed into his Way of the Cross, he returned to embrace his second and great baptism on Calvary. He spoke of his destiny in Jerusalem when he said, "There is a baptism with which I must be baptized, and how great is my anguish until it is accomplished" (Luke 12: 50). If you accept the challenge he extended to those who wished to follow him — "take up your cross and follow me" — then at this moment you are also walking your way of the cross to your second and great baptism, to your own death.

A Pilgrim's Prayer of the Road

O Lord of the Cross,
>   you know that the first days of cross carrying
>   are not always difficult.
Self-esteem can be found in its great challenge,
>   legitimate pride in heroically bearing its weight,
>   or secret pride when it is an invisible painful cross.
But as the hard road of life lengthens, we become weary;
>   shifting its weight, we beg you to take our cross away.

O Jesus, were you ever tempted to discard your cross,
>   and drop its ugly burden of shame and disgrace?
It seems you saw your cross as a sign of divine favor;
>   help me likewise to embrace my cross.
Like one who is blind to fear, may I take up my cross
>   as an essential element of my destiny toward holiness
>   and the holiness of the world,
>   with which it is intermingled.

+

Let me take up my cross and follow you, Lord Jesus,
for by doing so I share in the liberation of the world.

PILGRIMAGE SUNDAY
The First Sunday in Lent

It is customary on group pilgrimages to occasionally provide pilgrims with free days to spend as they wish. On our pilgrimage we will have days when there will be no scheduled visits to shrines made sacred by the passion of Christ. Touring pilgrims often use such days to visit interesting historical sites not included in the itinerary.

A VISIT TO THE WADI QELT

We praise you and we follow you, O Christ,
because by our crosses united, we redeem the world.

Today we take a side trip to visit the Monastery of St. George on the Wadi Qelt. (A *wadi* is a rocky creek bed that is dry except during the rainy season.) We leave the main Jerusalem-Jericho road shortly after the Almog Junction (*see map on page 22*) and walk to our right along a rocky, narrow road that leads to the monastery. The road soon shrinks to a mere pathway with carved steps that lead down to a steep canyon of yellow-gray limestone walls rising above the wadi. As we move along the dry creek bed, looking up we can see numerous cave entrances in the walls of the canyon with a white cross crudely painted beside each entrance. A millennium or more ago these small natural canyon caves were inhabited by hundreds of hermits living reclusive lives of prayer.

Soon we can make out the small stone monastery of St. George perched halfway up the face of the cliff. Climbing the narrow winding path up the canyon wall, we arrive at the front gate of this Greek Orthodox monastery named after St. George of Koziba. It was built in the fifth century on top of a previously

existing fourth century oratory used for the Sunday Divine
Liturgy by the hermits whose abandoned caves we just passed.
Entering the monastery's small chapel, a black-robed monk
proudly shows us the skulls of the fourteen monks who were
slaughtered by fifth-century Persians. After that disaster this
holy place was abandoned until the twelfth-century Crusades,

when attempts were made to restore the monastery. Those efforts at rebuilding failed — as was noted by a pilgrim like yourself who in 1483 wrote in his journal that all he saw when he visited here was ruins. The Greek Orthodox Church, whose small handful of monks maintains this shrine, began the restoration of the present monastery in 1878.

One reason why this monastery has long been a favorite pilgrimage destination is that by tradition it marks the site of a cave where the Old Testament prophet Elijah stayed on his way to Mount Sinai as he fled for his life. Christian custom also contends that Joachim, the father of Mary of Nazareth, came to this cave to pray that God might heal the infertility that cursed him and his wife Anna. Tradition has it that in his prayer an angel announced to him the good news of the conception of his daughter Mary. Visiting this site is a good preparation for some of the future stops in our pilgrimage. Together, these sacred spots will resemble a many-tiered wedding cake celebrating various historical events that took place in this same general location.

Leaving the monastery, we will return to the main Jericho-Jerusalem road. As we do, reflect upon the seemingly impossible situations that faced Elijah and Joachim. Both carried personal crosses as their share in the divine plan of global redemption. While the conflicts in their personal lives must have seemed impossible to resolve, as the angel told Mary, "With God all things are possible" (Luke 1: 37).

On this day, dedicate with faith your personal lifelong pilgrimage — regardless of how insignificant it may seem to you — as an important part of God's liberation of the world. Conclude your dedication by tracing upon yourself the sign of the cross with the words, "With + God + all things + are possible."

+

Let me take up my cross and follow you, Lord Jesus.
for by doing so I share in the liberation of the world.

THE FIFTH DAY OF THE PILGRIMAGE

Monday of the First Week in Lent

THE SECOND STATION
THE ROAD UP TO JERUSALEM

We praise you and we follow you, O Christ,
because by our crosses united, we redeem the world.

Scripture Reading for the Second Station

After John had been arrested, Jesus came to Galilee proclaiming the
gospel of God: "This is the time of fulfillment. The kingdom of God is
at hand. Repent, and believe in the good news." —Mark 1: 14-15

This dusty journey from Jericho up to Jerusalem embodies the
daily journey of Jesus with his baptismal cross. His true cross
was his personal struggle to live out the gospel of God as he
went about announcing the good news of God's love to all who
would listen. By living, without compromise, God's embodiment

in his flesh, he would incur the vicious wrath of Jerusalem's religious hierarchy and Rome's imperial power. These two giant institutions of power, along with those who controlled the wealth and land, were determined to prevent the arrival of his announced time of God's justice for the poor and oppressed.

The Road from Jericho to Jerusalem

Be aware that the road to Jerusalem is a precarious path of choices. You can't walk it without having to choose which side of the road you will travel on: One lane is taken by the powerful of this earth; on the other side walk the powerless ones of the world. Jesus said that we cannot serve two masters, so in life you must decide over and over again with whom you will cast your lot. Choose with caution, for what appears to be the wrong side of the road is the side consistently chosen by God. Like those abandoned prayer caves along the canyon walls of the Wadi Qelt, find your own prayer cave so that you can make the right choices in life. The Way of the Cross is the Way of Choice, and at each crossroad we must again face a cross of decision.

Do not be anxious; rather, be confident and hopeful. For,

like Jesus, you also have been given not only your cross but also the gift of the Holy Spirit. At each crossroad, God's Spirit is eager to guide you in making the right choice.

Crossroad Prayer

O Holy Spirit Adviser, Divine Wisdom,
    my baptismal Counselor dwelling within,
    whisper your directions, point the way.
Embolden me to choose your way,
    even when it goes uphill,
    and never to take the easy road
    of compromises and social concessions.

Help me to discern the clever propaganda
    of government, business and the world,
    used to sway my judgments and decisions.
Rather, may I always choose
    your crossroad that leads to life
    and never detour off my Way of the Cross.

+

*Let me take up my cross and follow you, Lord Jesus,
for by so doing I share in the liberation of the world.*

The Sixth Day of the Pilgrimage

Tuesday of the First Week in Lent

Meditation at Mount Maale Adumin

*We praise you and we follow you, O Christ,
because by our crosses united, we redeem the world.*

Approximately halfway from Jericho (*see map on page 22*) the road begins to ascend; to the left is a mountain named *Maale Adumin*, the Red Ascent, because of its reddish tint. On the right is a sixteenth century Turkish building, which Christian pilgrims call "the Inn of the Good Samaritan." Luke's Gospel records that Jesus told twenty-four parables, seventeen of them on his journey to Jerusalem. By means of parables like "The Good Samaritan" he provided doorways for us to the Kingdom of God.

The entire life of Jesus was itself a living parable that told of God's healing mercy, of joyous table association with social outcasts and sinners, and of mercy-soaked pardon for all who had sinned. As God's Word incarnate, Jesus expressed the flamboyant presence of God in the midst of daily human struggles and God's communion with our joys and pleasures. Our pilgrimage from Jericho up to Jerusalem symbolizes the entire post-baptismal Galilean journey of Jesus, during which he generously lived out the implications of his baptism in the Holy Spirit.

We are called to live out our baptism in Christ with the same generosity. Indeed, heroism is required to tend to those wounded and cast into the ditch by the injustices and inequalities of the world. When it is not just a single person who is in need of compassionate care but hundreds of thousands, we can easily sit back and await the arrival of a divine savior. The pious temptation to wait for the Second Coming of Christ to bring peace and justice to our wounded earth prevents you and me from *becoming* the Coming of Christ!

Here at the shrine of the Inn of the Good Samaritan, ponder what it means to become a lifelong parable of the Good Christian. Such a disciple will stop by the roadside to help the afflicted, regardless of their race, class or religion. To all those tempted to wait for the Second Coming, Christ the Cross Carrier says, "Take up your cross of seeing me in every ditch, prison and soup line, and by your cross-vision join me in healing your world."

+

Let me take up my cross and follow you, Lord Jesus,
for by so doing I share in the liberation of the world.

THE SEVENTH DAY OF THE PILGRIMAGE
Wednesday of the First Week in Lent

MEDITATION AT THE MOUNT OF OLIVES

We praise you and we follow you, O Christ,
because by our crosses united, we redeem the world.

At sunrise on this new day in our pilgrimage we stand atop the Mount of Olives, which towers over the Holy City just to the west of it. After passing through the stark barrenness of the Jordan desert, our senses are now greeted with the fragrant silver-green of olive trees. In the spring this mountain ridge is blanketed with wind-rippled waves of blooming wildflowers. This morning, the warm lemon light of the rising sun washes the golden crown of the Mosque of the Rock as well as the red-tiled roofs of the stone buildings and the gray walls of the Old City.

A View of the Old City from the Mount of Olives

Looking down on the shimmering green crowns of the olive trees at the lower elevations of the mount is the Garden of Gethsemane. Rising out of the olive trees are the spires and domes of various churches clustered on the holy mount. Particularly striking is the Russian Orthodox Church of St. Mary Magdalene, with its seven gilded onion domes. About halfway down the mount is the church named *Dominus Flevit*, The Lord Wept, which commemorates the site where Jesus wept over the Holy City and her people for their failure to recognize the time of God's visitation.

From this point you can also see that the Mount of Olives road descends sharply westward down into the Kidron Valley. At the base of the valley are located the tombs of the prophets Hagai, Zechariah and Malachi. Because of the prophecy of Zechariah (chapter 14), our Jewish brethren believe that the Messianic era and its resurrection of the dead will begin here at the foot of the Mount of Olives. To the left are numerous

The Mount of Olives and Jewish Graves in the Foreground of the Old City

THE MOUNT OF OLIVES

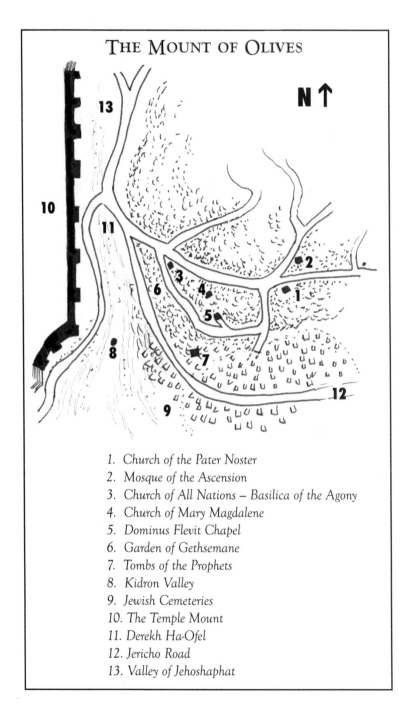

1. Church of the Pater Noster
2. Mosque of the Ascension
3. Church of All Nations – Basilica of the Agony
4. Church of Mary Magdalene
5. Dominus Flevit Chapel
6. Garden of Gethsemane
7. Tombs of the Prophets
8. Kidron Valley
9. Jewish Cemeteries
10. The Temple Mount
11. Derekh Ha-Ofel
12. Jericho Road
13. Valley of Jehoshaphat

Jewish cemeteries along the southern slopes of the Mount of Olives, for this place has been considered sacred since early times. It was from the top of the Mount of Olives that Jesus of Nazareth rode a donkey down into the Holy City through a turbulent sea of waving palm branches and thundering shouts of *hosanna*! By this deliberate act he boldly declared himself to be the humble, nonviolent King of Kings, following God's design that the Messiah would be devoid of royal trappings and weapons of power. It was also from here on this mount that he sent two disciples into Jerusalem to prepare for his Passover Last Supper, the Messianic Meal of the Cross.

Reflection

This pilgrimage road symbolically connects Jesus' baptism to the Meal of the Cross, which, like the first Messianic Meal, was a remembrance of liberation. The Passover meal celebrates God's redemption-liberation of the Hebrews from slavery in Egypt, and each Lord's Supper is a renewal of our liberation in Baptism. It reminds us that we are a community of disciples, who — as we will pray each day on this pilgrimage — join our crosses together for the redemption of the world.

Your cross, as it is unique to you, can seem to be private and individual. However, a central act of the Lord's Supper is Holy Communion, which, beyond being a communion with Christ, is a fusion of the crosses of all gathered about the table. The Eucharist nourishes cross carriers with the Bread of Life so they can gracefully carry their personal crosses. As this holy meal incorporates us into the Body of Christ, it also cross-invests us with the crosses of all his disciples. Whatever suffering is lacking in one is supplemented by the struggles of another, as together with Christ we restore the world in God's image.

+

Let me take up my cross and follow you, Lord Jesus, for by so doing I share in the liberation of the world.

THE EIGHTH DAY OF THE PILGRIMAGE
Thursday of the First Week in Lent

THE THIRD STATION
THE LAST SUPPER

We praise you, O Christ, and we follow you,
because by our crosses united, we redeem the world.

Scripture Reading for the Third Station

When the day of the Feast of the Unleavened Bread arrived, the day for sacrificing the Passover lamb, he sent out Peter and John, instructing them, "Go and make preparations for us to eat the Passover." They asked him, "Where do you want us to go to make the preparations?" And he answered them, "When you go into the city, a man will meet you carrying a jar of water. Follow him into the house that he enters...." —Luke 22: 7-10

This station is a logical destination along the way we have taken because each baptismal celebration is a memory shrine of the

Last Supper, where the death and resurrection is enfleshed in the living presence of the Risen One. Turning to our left as we descend the Mount of Olives, we again pass along the road that runs past the southern wall of the Holy City. In Peter and John's footsteps we approach *Wadi 'er Rababi*, which once was the site of the stinking, smoldering city dump called *Gehenna*, which Jesus compared to the hellish place of punishment.

Jesus told his two disciples to follow a man carrying a water jar into the city. Our path crosses the Kidron Valley where the *Gihon* Spring was located, the water source and very lifeblood of the ancient Holy City — for in ancient times it was the area's only reliable spring. It is approached down a flight of steps and through a stone arch. This would be a good spot for the two disciples to wait for a man with a water jar so they could follow him to the house with an upper room. Leaving the Spring of Gihon and returning to *Maale Ha-Shalom* Road, we approach the Zion Gate but do not enter the Holy City.

Turning to our left, we walk up toward Mount Zion on the southwestern side of the city, passing a building reverenced by Christian pilgrims as the house of the high priest Caiaphas. Continuing beyond a jog in the street and proceeding south, we come to one of the most sacred shrines of Jerusalem, the Cenacle — from the Latin *coenaculum*, "a dining hall." To pilgrims this holy site is better known as the Upper Room, the place where Jesus and his disciples ate his Last Supper.

> *While they were eating, he took bread, said the blessing, broke it and gave it to them, saying, "Take it; this is my body." Then he took the cup, gave thanks, and gave it to them, and they all drank from it. He said to them, "This is my blood of the covenant, which will be shed for many. Amen, I say to you, I shall not drink again of the fruit of the vine until the day I drink it new in the kingdom of God." —Mark 14: 22-25*

On the building is a pointed-arch entrance that leads to the place of the Last Supper. Passing through the archway, we

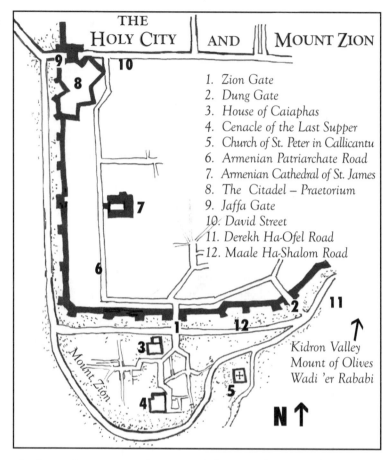

1. Zion Gate
2. Dung Gate
3. House of Caiaphas
4. Cenacle of the Last Supper
5. Church of St. Peter in Callicantu
6. Armenian Patriarchate Road
7. Armenian Cathedral of St. James
8. The Citadel – Praetorium
9. Jaffa Gate
10. David Street
11. Derekh Ha-Ofel Road
12. Maale Ha-Shalom Road

Kidron Valley
Mount of Olives
Wadi 'er Rababi

Mount Zion

N ↑

climb up the steps to the second floor and enter a large room with Gothic-style pillars that support a vaulted roof. This structure isn't the original room but was constructed in the Crusaders' time at the traditional site of the Last Supper. The original site most likely was on the roof, above the ceiling of this vaulted room. There, an open-air terrace overlooking the city's roofs would have allowed guests to enjoy the evening breezes and the full moon of the Passover.

At this station, we pause to remember the Meal of the Cross at which Jesus anticipated his death on Calvary. Here was celebrated the New Seder Supper, where just as the enslaved

Israelites had been freed from Egypt, God would again, with unconditional generosity, liberate those enslaved by evil. As the shadow of the cross eclipsed Jesus' baptism — and ours — that same dark shadow falls across the table of the Last Supper.

Each time the Lord's Supper, the Holy Eucharist, is celebrated, we become pilgrims of memory. Paradoxically, it is this Holy Meal of Remembrance and not the cross that is *the* sign of our Christian faith. Just as the road from Jesus' baptism led directly to the table of this upper room, so our baptisms lead us not only to *attend* the Eucharist of the Lord's Supper but also to *become* the Eucharist, to give away our body and blood in all we do.

Remembrance Prayer

"Remember me when you break bread."
Baptismal believers are faithful to these dying words,
   this Last Will of their beloved Lord,
   when they are fully present in what they do,
   investing their body and blood with love,
   their time and energies, their very selves,
   in life-giving deeds of generous love.

Christ's words echo in every Eucharist heart:
   Remember me at every altar table meal.
Remember me whenever you share any meal,
   for all food is a communion of God's love,
   and holy is all sharing in love and friendship.
Remember me with love, for I am truly present
   as you invest yourself in every work and task,
   in all that you do.
Do this — do everything — in memory of me.

+

Let me take up my cross and follow you, Lord Jesus,
for by so doing I share in the liberation of the world.

THE NINTH DAY OF THE PILGRIMAGE
Friday of the First Week in Lent

MEDITATION WHILE LINGERING
IN THE UPPER ROOM

We praise you and we follow you, O Christ,
because by our crosses united, we redeem the world.

The Upper Room is empty of furnishings, fixtures or religious appointments, yet because the Last Supper of Jesus was eaten here, it is a sacred shrine. Lacking pews, altar, cross, statues or stained glass windows, this vacant room is reverenced as the site of history's most famous and holy dinner.

The Upper Room

I propose that Jesus never intended that this Upper Room become a single, static shrine to his meal of the outpouring of God's love! Inspired by the Holy Spirit, he told his disciples, "Do this in memory of me," as he envisioned millions upon millions of table shrines in every land, not simply this single sacred space in the Holy Land. Every family table in the world where love is poured out in preparing and sharing a meal is an Upper Room shrine. Every table in any cafe or restaurant where friends gather in love is an Upper Room shrine. Every place where love is poured out in caring for the sick or assisting the oppressed and the needy is an Upper Room shrine. The unreligious environment of this room proclaims loudly a gospel dogma that it is in just such unchurchy places that we baptized pilgrims remember and make Christ present by investing ourselves in whatever we do. While the Lord's Supper is ritually celebrated inside church space, it is truly embodied in the tens of thousands of places where love is given away.

Recall that candidates desiring baptism first leave their old world and, after being baptized, enter into another world. Our third day at the Station of the Supper reveals this other world where those baptized and anointed in Christ act as the priestly people of God by consecrating all they touch into the living Eucharist of God's love. At a Seder table in this room, the disciples gathered as the New Family of God, born of water and Spirit; they belonged now to a family besides that of their blood and birth.

In addition to a cross, the Master asked his disciples to take his yoke upon their shoulders. We pilgrims, then, carry both a cross and a yoke, and at this station the two fuse into one. A yoke controls the lives of people as well as beasts. In the first-century world, wealthy landowners and the powerful harshly ruled the lives of poor peasant tenant farmers. Indeed, such oppressive yokes exist in every age. By contrast, Jesus says that his yoke is easy. Baptism into Christ places a yoke, a new way of life, upon us — one that is radically different from the yokes that society, business and religion place on our shoulders. Christ's yoke is a lifestyle of loving, a generous and joyful giving of yourself as food to others. This station could, thus, be called the Yoke Shrine, the world's greatest temple to Love, for the Lord's Supper completes our initiation into a lifestyle of love and nourishes us

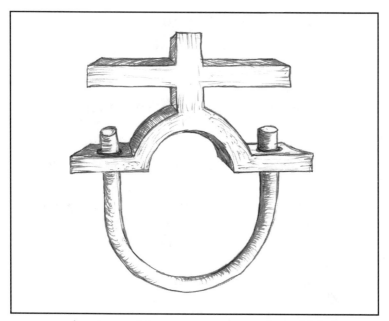

so we can live it out. Moreover, every act of unselfish love is a cross-infused deed that liberates both those who love and those loved. Faith in God's chemistry of the yoke-cross is required to trust that evil in our world will be removed not by the sword or by making laws, but only by that selflessly generous love that liberates with the power of the cross.

Two signs rest upon every expression of affection, the sign of the Cross and the sign of the Supper, which combine as a single redeeming celebration of God's love.

Scripture of Departure from the Upper Room

After singing a hymn, they went out to the Mount of Olives. Then Jesus said to them, "All of you will have your faith shaken, for it is written, 'I will strike the shepherd, and the sheep will be dispersed.'"
—Mark 14: 26-27

✝

Let me take up my cross and follow you, Lord Jesus, for by so doing I share in the liberation of the world.

Saturday of the First Week in Lent

THE ROAD TO THE GARDEN OF GETHSEMANE

We praise you and we follow you, O Christ,
because by our crosses united, we redeem the world.

Departing from the Upper Room down the steps, we again enter the street. This pilgrimage walk would ideally be at night, since it was nighttime when Jesus and his three closest disciples traveled this same route. Walking along the darkened street, we retrace our steps back toward the Zion Gate and make our way along the Maale Ha-Shalom Road that leads eastward toward the dark form of the Mount of Olives (*see map on page 55*).

The road to Gethsemane is the Way of Betrayal and Denial haunted by the memory of Jesus' exchanges with Judas and Simon Peter back in the Upper Room. Privately, Jesus had confronted Judas, who was about to betray him, and he predicted that Peter the Rock would deny him three times before the next dawn. This is a road shrine intended for all those who have been betrayed by people they trusted. Pause a moment on this road of treachery and exercise your baptismal priestly power, granting forgiveness and absolution to your betrayers for their unfaithfulness. If you have never been betrayed by someone you loved and trusted, then this is the place to say a prayer of gratitude for being spared that heart-piercing pain.

This road that leads to the Olive Garden is an avenue of agony and dread. On that fateful night the Shepherd Jesus walked this same road, anticipating the painful blow about to strike him down, gripped by the anguish that would be caused by the cowardly desertion of his friends. As darkness filled the night, so an intense ebony sadness must have overwhelmed his heart. Walking quietly beside him were his closest friends, Peter, James and John, each of whom had just boldly avowed their heroic defense of Jesus. Yet, gripped by the fear of death, they soon would flee from him into the darkness.

This innocent-looking road to Gethsemane is part of the Via Dolorosa, the Way of Sorrows, even though it lies outside the walls of the Holy City. Each of us, as a pilgrim of the cross, has or will have to travel this avenue of anticipated agony. It will lead not to Gethsemane, but perhaps down some hospital hallway to surgery or to the boss's office where you'll be told you are being discharged. It may be the drive leading you to divorce court or to the bedside of a dying spouse and life companion. May retracing this road to the garden in prayer and imagination prepare us to walk our personal ways of anticipated agony. May we embrace the trust in God's abiding care for us that Jesus embodied on his walk to Gethsemane.

Having reached the southeast corner of the Temple Mount, we take a shortcut, as Jesus must have done, descending into the stony Kidron Valley. From there we climb to the garden of olive trees whose leaves are now etched in silver by the pale moonlight. We have now arrived at the scene of the Fourth Station of the Cross, the Garden of Gethsemane.

+

Let me take up my cross and follow you, Lord Jesus,
for by so doing I share in the liberation of the world.

The Second Sunday in Lent

You may wish to spend this free day reflecting on the scripture readings for this Lenten Sunday or, if you desire, take a brief side trip to visit the Church of the Pater Noster located here on the Mount of Olives.

THE CHURCH OF THE PATER NOSTER

We praise you and we follow you, O Christ,
because by our crosses united, we redeem the world.

Walking up the road leading to Bethphage, on your right is the world's largest and oldest Jewish cemetery. After passing the side road on your left that leads to the Mosque of the Ascension (*see map on page 51*), we come upon the Church of

The Mount of Olives and Jewish Graves
in the Foreground of the Old City

the *Pater Noster*, Latin for "Our Father." The inside of this church is impressive; along its walls the Lord's Prayer is inscribed in seventy different languages, showing how universal is this prayer of Jesus.

The first church on this site was called the Church of the Disciples. It was constructed around the year 328 by order of Queen Helena, the mother of the Roman Emperor Constantine. The original church was built beside a cave, where tradition held that Jesus had taught his disciples his prayer now called the Our Father. This building was destroyed by the Persians in a war in 610 and rebuilt in 1106 by the Crusaders. After their departure from the Holy Land, the church crumbled into disrepair. It remained so until 1856 when the princess Aurella de la Tour d'Auvergne came upon this site while on a pilgrimage to Jerusalem. Distressed at finding it only a pile of rubble, she devoted a major part of her fortune and seventeen years of her life to rebuilding the church. The present structure reflects additional renovations begun in 1920.

A luxury for those on a leisurely pilgrimage is having the time to sit and rest a while at shrines. We will enjoy such a respite in the restored ancient cave grotto where tradition says Jesus actually taught his prayer. Listening with the ears of your soul, you can hear ghosts of crusaders lingering about this Mount of Olives shrine, since the Pater Noster was their primary prayer. Before modern rosary beads were used to count Hail Marys, crusader knights daily prayed a rosary of the Lord's Prayer, using a cord strung with precious stones or simply with knots tied in a cord to serve as counters. Many common medieval folk adapted the custom of the Crusader's Pater Noster rosary as their daily prayer.

Generations of children have learned the Lord's Prayer directly from their parents. Indeed, after almost two millennia, this universal prayer of all Christians remains dynamically alive today. Yet like the previous churches that have stood on this site and fell into ruin, this ancient prayer of Jesus is not immune to damage and disrepair. Perhaps what most threatens the vitality of the Our Father is the routine of repetition. One slowly prayed Lord's Prayer is worth a thousand thoughtlessly rattled off. As Princess Aurella spent the last years of her life restoring the tumbled-down Pater Noster Church, consider dedicating yourself with affection to the continuous renewal of the prayer itself.

Prayerfully descend from this cave grotto into the cave of your heart and slowly, soulfully pray this gift from Jesus. As you pray, "your will be done, on earth as it is in heaven," pause to remember your personal cross, which you symbolically carried up this hillside as part of our pilgrimage. Your unique cross is essential to God's design for your salvation and to your participation in the liberation of all humanity. Your cross is no curse. It is the cross-construction tool with which you can contribute to building up the reign of God.

In saying, "give us this day our daily bread," linger on the word "daily." This prayer of prayers reminds us not to be anxious about storing away bread, supplies, money or other resources for our tomorrows, but rather to be satisfied with today's bread. Prudence requires us to be concerned about our future, to make appropriate plans and preparations, but not to do so with anxiety. Rather, our Lord told us to live with abiding trust, because our Divine Parent has adopted us by our watery birth and will care for our daily needs.

"Forgive us our trespasses," is Jesus' call to a lavish generosity in gifting others with our pardon. Whenever we pray this phrase, we make a contractual agreement stating our desire to accept the divine arrangement to be forgiven by God according to the measure we use to forgive others. Formidable, then, are these words, since any failure to grant pardon to another holds dire consequences for us.

"Lead us not into temptation…" concludes the Lord's Prayer.

Located just below this church is the Garden of Gethsemane where Jesus wrestled with his great temptation to flee from this moment of truth. His sweat-and-blood prayer was that he might be spared not simply the pain of his passion but also the cup of his destiny offered to him by God. That cup held a shameful, torturous death wrapped in the disgrace of being excommunicated from his Jewish faith. He embraced that cup of fate with a trusting faith that his seemingly insignificant death alongside common criminals held cosmic consequences for how the world was to be healed by his beloved God. Your cup of destiny is likewise essential in God's strategy to heal and renew the world. Drink it with confident trust.

Also, realize that God never leads you into sin's enticement, because the Divine Mystery never leads you anywhere! God has given you the greatest of all gifts, the freedom of choice. Every time some evil beguiles you, you are given a choice — and the Spirit's grace — to prove your love by being faithful to God, even unto the point of death.

It is time to depart from this sacred site and descend the hill toward the next station on our Pilgrimage Way of the Cross, the Garden of Temptation.

+

Let me take up my cross and follow you, Lord Jesus,
for by so doing I share in the liberation of the world.

THE ELEVENTH DAY OF THE PILGRIMAGE

Monday of the Second Week in Lent

THE FOURTH STATION

THE AGONY IN THE GARDEN OF GETHSEMANE

We praise you and we follow you, O Christ,
because by our crosses united, we redeem the world.

Scripture for the Fourth Station

Then Jesus came with them to a place called Gethsemane, and he said to his disciples, "Sit here while I go over there and pray...." Then he said to them, "My soul is sorrowful even to death. Remain here and keep watch with me." He advanced a little and fell prostrate in prayer, saying, "My Father, if it is possible, let this cup pass from me; yet, not as I will, but as you will." —Matthew 26: 36, 38-39

This olive grove is called Gethsemane, from *Gat Shmanim*, meaning "oil press," and it was here that Jesus agonized in prayer and was arrested. Today a large church stands on the accepted site of his dark night of prayerful suffering and arrest. On the front wall of the church known as the Church of All Nations or the Basilica of the Agony is a beautiful façade in glistening golden mosaic depicting Jesus taking upon himself the sufferings of the world. Among the numerous shrines of

Church of All Nations

the Holy City, this is the newest, having been built as recently as 1924 over the site of earlier church-shrines dating back to the fourth century. Around 720, an earthquake destroyed the original church, which was replaced by another that was abandoned in the fourteenth century. Each of the churches has revered a large stone upon which Jesus is supposed to have knelt and prayed on the night of his arrest.

Instead of entering the basilica, let's walk across the road to a private section of this olive garden that is usually restricted. Because the gate is unlocked today, we can enter this old part of the grove containing aged gnarled olive trees, some of which are said to be hundreds of years old. Here, rather than inside the church building, one can experience what Gethsemane must have looked like 2,000 years ago when Jesus came here to pray. Overhead, the twisting tree branches form a leafy roof, creating a simple, rustic hermitage. As with our walk from the Upper Room two days ago, the best time to visit this site is in the darkness of night. Pause and absorb the mystery of this holy hideaway, Jesus' secret place of prayer, where he came on the night before his death. Envision silver shafts of moonlight creating a latticework of light and darkness within which he agonizes over his approaching betrayal and excruciating passion.

This spring-equinox moonlit olive garden became God's Gat Shmanim, the divine "oil press" in which the oil of loyalty was pressed out of Jesus like oil from olives. A short distance up the hill from here, he taught his disciples to pray for God's will to be done. Upon the gnarled stone of this garden, as upon an altar, he consecrated his words of prayer, pouring them into his own flesh and blood, his sweat and tears.

At each previous station of the cross we have prayed, "We praise you and we follow you, O Christ." At this station those words uncomfortably lodge in our throat. We fear having to follow him to this place. Agonizing is the act of transforming the words of prayer into a living prayer by giving priority to

Grove of Olive Trees in the Garden of Gethsemane

God's will over our own. Like the three chosen disciples, you and I typically dread facing physical pain and emotional suffering. We are paralyzed by moments of truth and are prone to flee from them whenever possible. Yet God's Gethsemane is not a garden for growing olives but rather for cultivating heroes and heroines. This Station of Holy Gethsemane is not found just in the Holy City of Jerusalem. It is also located in any home or hospital, in any time of crisis and decision, any place of sacrifice and suffering.

Your personal pilgrimage of the cross began at your baptism, which is in reality a birthing bath of heroes called to live out God's enfleshment in our times of crisis and challenge. Jesus was birthed not only in Bethlehem, but even more so at the Jordan River in his baptism into his awesome mission of being God's love in human flesh. He lived out his rebirth by allowing God-in-his-flesh to enjoy table meals with sinners and outcasts, by healing those crippled of heart and spirit, and opening eyes blind to God's radically new and different way of responding to injury, war and sin. Those baptized into his death and resurrection also share his mission of being God's love in their flesh, with all the consequences flowing from such an astonishing reality.

The Gethsemane cup he so earnestly pleaded might pass him by was the cup of the consequences of being God's love in human flesh, the divine light in the darkness. As Jesus knelt weeping his prayer, he could feel that the evil powers of darkness were already surging around him and that the moment of his betrayal was at hand. The dark, diabolical forces of the official religious institution and the reigning government of Imperial Rome were already on their way to this hidden place of prayer to arrest him. The events about to unfold were only the harvest of his efforts to live out the implications of his baptism. When you and I live as fully as possible our baptismal mystery of God enfleshed in our bodies — by loving even our enemies, by never judging others, by never returning injury for injury and never failing to forgive — we also will have to reap the harvest of our baptism.

"Not as I will, but as you will," is a statement of surrender that can only come from a humble heart. Jesus told us to learn a lesson from him, for he was meek and humble of heart, and the consequences of that lesson of humility were revealed here in Gethsemane. Authentic humility involves surrendering to the ugly, unexplainable mystery of why Evil is allowed to triumph in this world. Daily living the lesson of authentic humility also implies allowing the dark forces of disease and old age to diminish and destroy you while you trust that in the end God will restore you to an even greater abundance of life.

At this Fourth Station, pray for the grace to be able to surrender. Ask for the gift to raise your hands, not in giving up but with a profound trust in the mysterious ways of God. We place our faith in the Divine Consecrator, the One who endlessly transforms evil into good, darkness into light and death into life.

Gethsemane Prayer

O agonizing Lord of Gethsemane,
    when I am tempted to resist my cup of pain,
    show me how to surrender lovingly
    to the mysteriously loving ways of God.

Imitating your prayer, I am not ashamed
    to ask that my cup of pain pass me by,
    fearful that I lack the courage to drink it,
    dreading the agony that it will cause me.

Transplant in me your humble heart
    so I can heroically surrender to Love,
    joining my personal cross with yours,
    as together we drink your cup of tears.

So Judas got a band of soldiers and guards from the chief priests and Pharisees and went to the garden with lanterns, torches and weapons. Jesus...said to them, "Whom are you looking for?" They answered him, "Jesus the Nazarene." He said to them, "I AM."

                                                           –John 18: 3-5

+

Let me take up my cross and follow you, Lord Jesus, for by so doing I share in the liberation of the world.

Tuesday of the Second Week in Lent

MEDITATION ON THE WAY
TO THE HOUSE OF THE HIGH PRIEST

We praise you and we follow you, O Christ,
because by our crosses united, we redeem the world.

To follow the now-arrested Jesus to the place of his night trial, we return across the Kidron Valley to the Holy City by the same path we used to come here to Gethsemane *(see maps on pages 51 and 55)*. This would be the same route along which Jesus, the arrested criminal and troublemaker, was taken for his appearance before the court of the priests and elders. Again, this walk would ideally take place in the darkness of night. Walking in the dark is difficult — how much more when your hands are tied together with ropes, as were Jesus' on that night of his arrest. We are grateful that we are only pilgrims, and not prisoners like the Prisoner from Nazareth, who was roughly dragged into a darkness deeper and more sinister than the blackness of any night.

As we cross the ravine, on the left are the tombs of the Jewish prophets. The northern end of this Kidron Valley is named the Valley of *Jehoshaphat*, the Hebrew for, "God Shall Judge." Did the prophet Jesus ponder his own death and burial as he passed these tombs of dead prophets like Zechariah and Malachi? Unlike them, he could not expect ever to have a tomb, because Roman criminals and Jewish heretics were tossed like garbage into a ditch or into a common mass grave. It was appropriate that this valley he was crossing was named God Shall Judge, since he was on his way to be judged by the high priests' religious court and then by the Roman judge, Pontius Pilate.

The Tombs of the Prophets in the Kidron Valley

Reflection

Whenever you are judged by the dark powers of gossip, prejudice or envy, or even by your religion or state, remember the name of this valley: God Shall Judge. Realize, too, that we are all addicts. All of us are addicted to playing God and passing judgment on others — on their motives and behaviors, their faults and weaknesses. Whenever you are so tempted to judge, recall the name of this valley: God Shall Judge. The day is approaching when you and I shall stand on trial before the judgment of God. Yet this divine judgment is not exclusively delayed until our death, for daily we are judged by our thoughts, intentions and actions. Be not afraid of your final day in court, however, if you are living out Jesus' joyful good news: "Stop judging and you will not be judged. Stop condemning and you will not be condemned. Forgive and you will be forgiven" (Luke 6: 37-38).

Having crossed over the Kidron Valley, we follow the road that makes its way beneath Temple Mount until we come to the

Dung Gate *(see map on page 55)*. Without entering the Holy City we pause to reflect that it was through the Dung Gate in the original old city walls that Jesus would have been taken to reach the residence of the High Priest. In Hebrew this gate is named *Sha'ar Ha'Ashpot,* "the Gate of Garbage." Thus, it was a most symbolic gateway for the Galilean prophet and prisoner Jesus to enter the Holy City. On that fateful night he walked the Way of Shame, where he would be treated as human garbage: slapped and spat upon, ridiculed and shamed, stripped of his clothing and then discarded.

The Way of Christ's Cross is often the Garbage Route, where those arrested for their beliefs or who cry out for justice and equality are treated like dung. Garbage stinks and is shunned; paradoxically, those who are most Godlike are also shunned. It's not the Godlike in the sense of being pious, but those who are like God in how they speak, judge and love. Those who strive to live in fidelity to the teachings of Jesus and refuse to bear arms or engage in war are often considered to be weaklings — or even the rubbish of society. Those who lift the veil of hypocrisy, exposing the lies and injustices in government, church and the corporate world are often discarded like trash. While our hearts dream of being heroic, we dread walking the Way of the Cross of Garbage.

After our reflection outside the Dung Gate, we continue up the road until we reach the Zion Gate, where we turn left and follow the street to the traditional site of the house of the High Priest Caiaphas. The Armenian Church of St. Savior is now located at this site where Jesus was taken after his arrest in Gethsemane and tried by the Sanhedrin. In the courtyard of this house was the place where Simon Peter denied Jesus three times before the cock crowed. Like the house of Caiaphas, the Church of St. Savior also has a large courtyard. The present church dates back to the twelfth century and was built over the ruins of a fifth-century church. It also is reverenced as the site of the cell in which Jesus was held overnight awaiting his trial by Pilate.

As is so typical in Jerusalem, another shrine is also revered as the site of Caiaphas' house. Located just down the hill, almost hidden in the trees, is the Roman Catholic Church of St. Peter in *Callicantu*, "at the Crowing of the Cock." Since Byzantine times it has been the alternate location of Peter's denial, and in the 1920s a beautiful church was built on it. Now, however, it is considered an unlikely site, since it would have been located outside of the original walls of Jerusalem at Jesus' time (the present walls were rebuilt in 1560 by Sultan Suleyman the Magnificent), and the High Priest would surely have resided within the Holy City (*see map on page 90*).

The Church of St. Savior marks the site of the Fifth Station of the Cross and so is a good place to go in and pray. The earth that lies beneath this stone floor is saturated with memories of a friend's betrayal. The soil stinks with the lies of false witnesses and Jesus' words twisted out of context, constituting the putrid sham of a religious court of justice.

+

Let me take up my cross and follow you, Lord Jesus,
for by so doing I share in the liberation of the world.

Wednesday of the Second Week in Lent

THE FIFTH STATION

THE TRIAL OF JESUS
BEFORE THE RELIGIOUS COURT

We praise you and we follow you, O Christ,
because by our crosses united, we redeem the world.

Scripture for the Fifth Station

The chief priests and the entire council kept trying to obtain testimony against Jesus in order to put him to death, but they found none.... The high priest rose before the assembly and questioned Jesus, saying, "Have you no answer?" But he was silent and answered nothing. Again the high priest asked him and said to him, "Are you the Messiah, the son of the Blessed One?" Then Jesus answered, "I am, and 'you will see the Son of Man seated at the right hand of the Power and coming with the

*clouds of heaven.'" At that the high priest tore his garments and said,
"What further need have we of witnesses?"* —Mark 14: 55, 60-63

Stand quietly at this place and absorb the anguish Jesus must
have felt at being judged and condemned by religious leaders
whom he had been raised to think of as God's vicars on earth.
Sadly, so often those who occupy the revered seats of religious
power are mere pious custodians of yesterday and vigilant
guardians of the status quo. As with the high priest Caiaphas,
their concern is for the welfare of the religious institution and
not for justice and the truth.

By the judgment of this religious court, Jesus — as a devout
Jew — was stripped of his membership among the Chosen People
of God, which was understood to sever him completely from
God's mercy. Being excommunicated, he would be denied the
consolation of a proper religious burial. Of the many crosses
Jesus carried to Calvary, one of the most excruciating crosses
placed upon him was being condemned and rejected by his
lifelong, beloved religion.

This pilgrimage shrine of the high priest's house is, indeed,
symbolic, for many are the disciples of Jesus who have been
tried before religious courts. This shrine is crowded with the
spirits of his first Jewish disciples who were dragged before
synagogue and temple courts. Also among the crowd of the
condemned standing in the shadows of this church are the
spirits of those throughout the ages who have defied religious
convention — history's many brave hearts like Joan of Arc,
mystics such as Meister Eckhart, religious reformers like Martin
Luther, along with theologians as great as St. Thomas Aquinas
and brilliant scientists such as Galileo. With them stand
countless unnamed others who, in the name of Christ, were
tortured by the Church's Inquisition, along with the thousands
of unfortunate women judged by religious authorities as witches
and burned at the stake. In the silence of this holy place, listen

and hear their mournful litany of the sufferings they shared with Jesus, the condemned prisoner of religion.

Fifth Station Prayer

The cross of Christ confronts all the powers of evil,
   the diabolic forces of hate, violence and war,
   the suffocating powers of greed and exploitation
   that grasp the reins of power over the powerless.

Blessed are the crosses married to the cross of Christ,
   for they share in his work of destroying evil by love.
The cross of Christ confronts camouflaged evils,
   hidden by piously masked groups and persons
   who quote scripture to justify their injustices.

The Cross reveals the evils of the Anti-Kingdom,
   whose diabolic agents nailed Jesus to his cross,
   and who do so again and again in age after age,
   to every disciple who refuses to desert his or her cross.

+

Let me take up my cross and follow you, Lord Jesus,
for by so doing I share in the liberation of the world.

THE FOURTEENTH DAY OF THE PILGRIMAGE
Thursday of the Second Week in Lent

MEDITATION AT THE COURTYARD
OF THE CHURCH OF SAINT SAVIOR

We praise you and we follow you, O Christ,
because by our crosses united, we redeem the world.

Scripture for the Fourteenth Day

One of the high priest's maids came along. Seeing Peter warming himself, she looked intently at him and said, "You too were with the Nazarene, Jesus." But he denied it, saying, "I neither know nor understand what you are talking about." So he went out into the outer court. (The cock crowed.) The maid saw him and began again to say to the bystanders, "This man is one of them." Once again he denied it. A little later the bystanders said to Peter once more, "Surely you are one of them; for you too are a Galilean." He began to curse and to swear, "I do not know this man about whom you are talking." And immediately the cock crowed a second time. Then Peter remembered the word that Jesus had said to him, "Before the cock crows twice, you will deny me three times." He broke down and wept.
—Mark 14: 66-72

This church at this stop on our pilgrimage could also be called the Church of Saint Peter and All Cowards. If you step outside the church, you will be standing in what was once the courtyard of the house of the high priest. At this place Simon Peter, who had followed his dear friend from the Garden of Gethsemane, also found himself on trial. The judge was not the high priest or any elder of the religious court but a common household maid and the bystanders gathered in the courtyard. Cowardly

Peter three times denied he even knew Jesus and attempted to completely disassociate himself from the prisoner being judged inside.

Simon Peter's courtroom was the high priest's courtyard, where he stood to testify that he was neither a friend nor a disciple of Jesus. Fearing for his life, Peter lied and gave false testimony — as did the other witnesses against Jesus inside the house. Then, as a rooster crowed, Peter remembered the prophecy of Jesus about his cowardly betrayal and fled the courtyard sobbing in grief.

Peter's courtyard trial is typical of the human courts where you and I are called to give testimony regarding our relationship with Jesus and his teachings. While we may not verbally deny him or his way of life, we often choose an even more cowardly position: silence. When trapped in discussions that contradict our Christian beliefs — perhaps conversations laced with the poison of prejudice against people of color, aliens and those of different religious or sexual orientations — we betray our Master by weakheartedly remaining silent. While we will not be executed for witnessing to our belief in the teachings of Jesus, we fear another type of dying, the painful death of being socially scorned and rejected.

This courtyard outside the Church of Saint Savior is crowded with the silent presence of thousands upon thousands of disciples of Simon Peter. Unlike the small group of invisible heroic witnesses that were inside the church, here outside in the courtyard is a vastly larger invisible crowd of cowards. Whether for reasons of respectability, profit, popularity or advancement, these multitudes have denied their crosses and their friendship with their Lord Jesus. By silence or by outright agreement with evil, they also have denied their consciences. Instead of being companions of the cross, they have become co-conspirators with evil.

Prayer to St. Peter

St. Peter, patron saint of cowards,
    at this unholy shrine of your betrayal
    help me honestly face my cowardice
    in failing to affirm the teachings of my Lord, Jesus,
    within the fabric of my daily life
    and, by my silence, denying my Teacher.

The Christ that lives in me must shudder
    at my unspoken consent to words of hate,
    my broken baptismal vow to reject Satan
    and all clever poisonous devices of evil,
    subtly aligning me with wicked forces
    and making Christ's presence impotent in me.

As your tears, Peter, were your saltwater baptism,
    may my tearful regret for being a coward
    plunge me again into Christ's death and rising,
    so when I next find myself confronted by evil,
    I may be a witness to Christ's love and his cross.
St. Peter, be my model of repentant reform.

+

Let me take up my cross and follow you, Lord Jesus,
for by so doing I share in the liberation of the world.

Visual Reflection

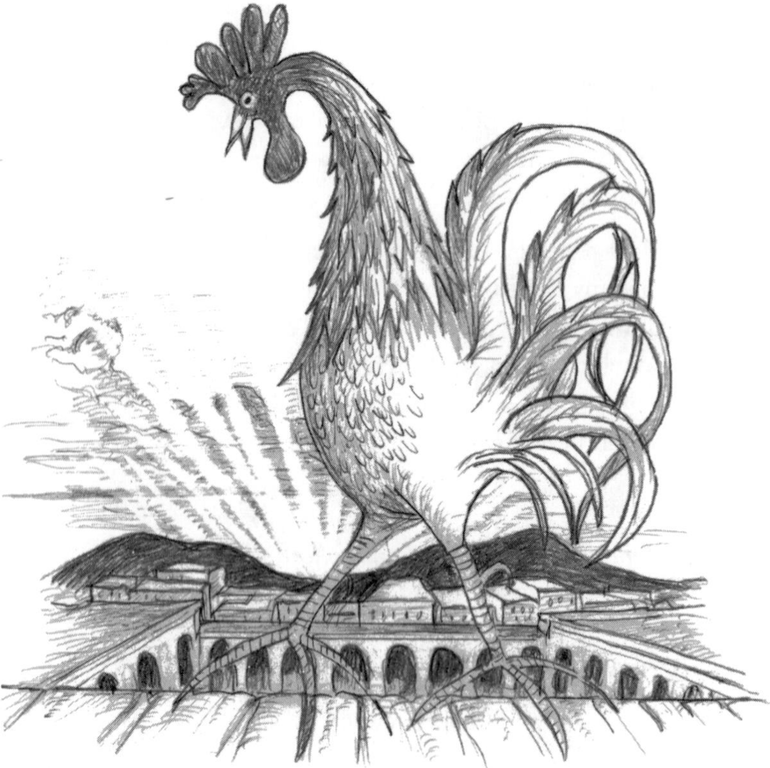

COCKSURE SIMON PETER

When Jesus told his friends of his approaching death and that their faith would be seriously shaken, Peter boasted with arrogance that, even if the others might abandon Jesus, he would never deny his beloved Lord. Jesus said in reply, "Peter, this very night before the cock crows twice you will deny me three times" (Mark 14: 30).

The Hebrews divided the night into four watches. The first was the beginning of the night, and the middle watch was at midnight. Predawn was the cock-crowing watch, and sunrise was the fourth watch. The Romans called the time before dawn *gallicinium*, the time when the cock crows. The rooster was a sacred bird to various ancient gods and was often used in antiquity for sacrifice. The cock was a particularly sacred bird to Apollo, the sun god, since it heralded the coming of the sun and was believed to drive off nocturnal demons. A popular symbol of vigilance, the rooster was used as a weathercock on church steeples and often appeared on grave markers. Yet St. Gregory suggested that the cock was a warning against arrogance. Perhaps he had Simon Peter in mind with this insight.

An Islamic legend tells of how on his Night Journey to heaven the Prophet Muhammad found in the first heaven a cock so enormous that its crest touched the second heaven. He said the crowing of this bird awakens every living creature except humans and predicted that when the cock ceases to crow, Judgment Day will be at hand. This prophecy certainly came true for Peter when the cock in Caiaphas' courtyard ceased crowing, for it signaled the time of his judgment as a coward and betrayer. Beset by guilt, he fled into the darkness, weeping uncontrollably.

In the years that followed, whenever Peter heard a cock crowing he surely must have awakened to the unconditional love and fidelity of his friend Jesus, whose rising from the tomb announced the beginning of an eternal new day. His cockiness transformed into wakefulness, Saint Peter has the rooster-like ability to awaken us daily to fidelity and unconditional love.

THE FIFTEENTH DAY OF THE PILGRIMAGE
Friday of the Second Week in Lent

THE SIXTH STATION
JESUS THE PRISONER

*We praise you and we follow you, O Christ,
because by our crosses united, we redeem the world.*

Scripture for the Sixth Station
*As soon as morning came, the chief priests with the elders and the
scribes...bound Jesus, led him away and handed him over to Pilate.*
—Mark 15: 1

The sham trial of Jesus was conducted at the priestly religious
court under the secrecy of nighttime darkness. The leaders and
elders condemned him to death, the fate of those who blaspheme
and make themselves equal with God. As a condemned prisoner,

Jesus would have had to be held overnight so that his accusers could take him the next morning to the Roman governor Pilate, whose authority was required to carry out their death decree. Tradition says that the cave prison cell in which Jesus was incarcerated overnight was located beneath the house of the high priest Caiaphas.

Descend now into the darkness of this black hole of a prison in which the condemned prisoner Jesus must have felt he was already entombed in a living death. This cave prison cell links the agony of Gethsemane with the anticipated passion and suffering along the Way of the Cross. Blaspheming carried a sentence of death by stoning, which the priestly court could have carried out, but death by crucifixion was possible only by an order of Pontius Pilate. The religious council had thus condemned Jesus to an excruciatingly shameful death, for the Romans crucified their victims naked on a cross and so totally visible to spectators. For a devout Jew like Jesus, this public nakedness would be as painful as actually dying. Being a condemned prisoner awaiting this shameful fate, his suffering must have also absorbed the pain of the disgrace that would be felt by his mother, family and friends at his execution. The scandal of his imminent, infamous death and the fear of guilt by association had already imprisoned his disciples in fear. In response, they had all already scattered like sheep before wolves.

He who was inspired by the Holy Spirit to call himself "the Light of the World" was now entombed in the sheer darkness of the pit of despair. Like centuries of prisoners of conscience who would come after him, Jesus was alone and abandoned — even, it seemed, by God. Had the Holy Spirit anticipated his imprisonment and inspired his parable about God's Last Judgment? In the parable, Jesus is a judge dividing the sheep from the goats. He says to those bound for paradise, "I was in prison and you visited me. Enter now into your everlasting reward." And those rewarded with Paradise say to

him, "Lord, when did we ever see you in prison and visit you?" As he ushers them into heaven, he says, "I solemnly say, whenever you visited the least of my brethren in prison you visited me" (Matthew 25: 36, 39-40).

This Sixth Station of the Cross is a sacred place for those, like Jesus, condemned to die by capital punishment. It is a shrine for all convicts and prisoners incarcerated in jails, penitentiaries and prison camps, for the Risen Christ resides with them.

Prison Prayer

O, Holy Convict Jesus, hear my prayer:
Cleanse me of my prejudice against convicts,
    my biased judgment that they are all guilty
    and so not deserving of justice or love,
    of pardon or a prodigal's welcome home.

Prisoner Jesus, condemned by two courts,
    cleanse us of our desire to punish criminals,
    seeking revenge for their crimes against us
    rather than their reform and reinstatement
    into the life of our community.

Ancient is our hunger for revenge
    against all public and private household crimes.
Convict Christ, let the image of your cross
    transform our lust for revenge into a love
    for those who cause us injury and pain.

+

Let me take up my cross and follow you, Lord Jesus,
for by so doing I share in the liberation of the world.

THE SIXTEENTH DAY OF THE PILGRIMAGE
Saturday of the Second Week in Lent

THE CITADEL — PILATE'S PALACE

We praise you and we follow you, O Christ,
because by our crosses united, we redeem the world.

Scripture for the Sixteenth Day

They bound him, led him away and handed him over to Pilate, the
governor. —Matthew 27: 2

Our pilgrimage now follows the way taken by the condemned
prisoner Jesus to be tried a second time, now by Pontius Pilate.
Leaving the residence of the high priest, we pass through the
Zion Gate *(see map on page 55)*, turn left and walk northward
down the Armenian Patriarchate Road. After passing Saint James
Cathedral on the right, we soon arrive at the stone fortress known
now as the Citadel, located just inside the Jaffa Gate.

The next three Stations of the Cross will take place at this
same location. Our Pilgrimage of the Cross differs from the
traditional Way of the Cross regarding the location of Jesus'
encounter with Pilate and the route he took to Calvary. At the
time of the original processions of the cross it was believed
that whenever the Roman governor visited Jerusalem he would
reside at the Roman Fortress Antonia, located near the Temple
of Herod. As a result, the customary Way of the Cross in
Jerusalem begins on the northeast side of the Holy City and
then follows the Via Dolorosa to the site of Calvary *(see map on*
page 16). Scholars today, however, are convinced that whenever
Pilate left his official residence at Caesarea to oversee security
on the occasions of the great festivals in Jerusalem he would

The Citadel

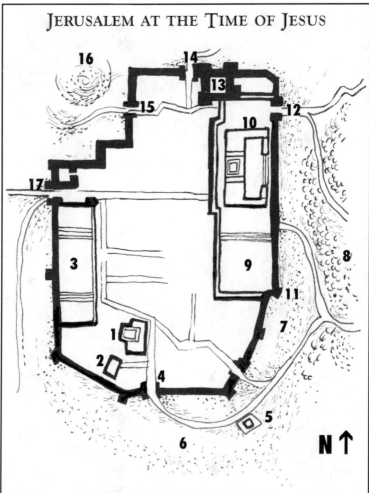

JERUSALEM AT THE TIME OF JESUS

1. Palace of the High Priests
   Annas and Caiaphas
2. Cenacle of the Last Supper
3. Palace of King Herod
4. Dung Gate
5. Siloam Pool
6. Valley of Gehenna
7. Kidron Valley
8. Garden of Gethsemane

9. The Temple Mount
10. The Temple of Herod
11. The Pinnacle of the Temple
12. The Golden Gate
13. The Fortress of Antonia
14. Gate of Benjamin
15. Gate of Ephraim
16. Golgotha
17. Jaffa Gate

stay at the former palace of King Herod the Great. This once-royal residence was located just inside the Jaffa Gate on the opposite side of the Old City, near the Western Wall. After King Herod's death his palace became the Praetorium of the Roman governors (*see replicas of Herod's Palace – the Praetorium – on page 92*). Today this site is called the Citadel or, in Arabic, *al-Qala'a*, and, according to modern scholarship, is the site at which Pontius Pilate judged and condemned Jesus to die on a cross.

Today nothing is left of Herod's palace – or any other part of the city of Jerusalem at the time of Jesus – except for the Western Wall of Herod's magnificent temple. What remains of the streets upon which Jesus of Nazareth carried his cross is now many feet below the present city, Jerusalem having been leveled to the ground at the end of the First Jewish War. During that Jewish uprising about thirty years after the death of Jesus, the Roman garrison took refuge in the towers of Herod's palace. The besieged, starved military garrison finally agreed to surrender to the rebelling Jewish Zealots. Instead of treating the surrendering troops as prisoners of war, however, the Jews massacred all of the unarmed legionnaires. Rome was so outraged that ten years later in 70 A.D., at the end of the victorious Roman siege of Jerusalem, the Roman Emperor ordered General Titus to level the city completely. Today, excavations beneath present-day Jerusalem have uncovered the foundations of Herod's palace, revealing that it was so massive as to have extended almost all the way to Mount Zion.

Mid Station Scripture

Then they brought Jesus from Caiaphas to the praetorium. It was morning. And they themselves did not enter the praetorium, in order not to be defiled so they could eat the Passover. So Pilate came out to them and said, "What charge do you bring against this man?" They answered, "If he were not a criminal we would not have handed him over to you." –John 18: 28-30

Replicas of Herod's Palace, later the Roman Praetorium

Prayer of the Religiously Pure
and Politically Correct

At this Roman court of judgment
   I cross-examine the evidence of my life.
Am I vigilant to carefully observe
   the minor legal obligations of my religion,
   while being guilty of the greater sin
   of falsely condemning others?
Like those who escorted Jesus here,
   am I a religious Jekyll and Hyde?

Do I choose what is proper and correct
   instead of doing what is right and just?
Am I like the politically prudent Pontius Pilate,
   ever-anxious about my career and future,
   playing the ancient game of evasion,
   dodging the demands of truth and justice?

If I judge myself guilty upon the evidence,
   may I repent and practice nonjudgment.
If the evidence of my life proves me innocent,
   then I have cause this day
   to rejoice in gratitude for God's grace
   that guides me daily along the path to God.

+

Let me take up my cross and follow you, Lord Jesus,
for by so doing I share in the liberation of the world.

THE WASHING
OF FEET

"Do this in memory of me." —Luke 22: 19 *(see also John 13: 15)*

The distance from the Cenacle's Upper Room to the Roman Praetorium is only a short walk, yet the washings at these two places are ten thousand miles apart. By washing his disciples' feet at the Last Supper, Jesus performs the holiest of rituals, becoming a responsible and humble servant. He then invites his disciples to do the same, "in memory of me." John's Gospel doesn't even mention Jesus' action of transforming bread and wine into his body and blood, one of the central realities of Christian faith; he instead places his Last Supper focus on the foot washing. For John, the act of washing feet is a Holy Eucharist, the Mass of Humble Service to God in others, an authentic sacrifice of love.

THE WASHING
OF HANDS

"I am innocent of this man's blood; look to it yourselves."
—*Matthew 27: 24*

The next day, a short distance away, Pontius Pilate echoes this action, washing his hands. Disclaiming his responsibility for condemning an innocent man to death, he chimes in with the voices of endless legions of corporate, institutional and civil servants: "I was only doing my duty." By choosing what was politically expedient, regardless of the trail of suffering involved in this choice, Pilate was acting as a responsible servant of the Institution. He is the patron sinner of all those who choose to be servants of any master other than the God of justice and love.

The Third Sunday in Lent

On this free day in our pilgrimage you can reflect upon the scripture readings for this Lenten Sunday or visit a nearby shrine.

A VISIT TO THE CATHEDRAL OF ST. JAMES

*We praise you and we follow you, O Christ,
because by our crosses united, we redeem the world.*

To visit this holy place we retrace our steps back down the Armenian Patriarchate Road, which led us to the Citadel (*see map on page 55*). This Armenian Catholic Cathedral is dedicated to James the Greater, the son of Zebadee and one of the intimate disciples of Jesus. Herod Agrippa executed him in 44 A.D., and this church is now located at the accepted site of his tomb.

Armenia, the cultural home of this church, was the first nation officially to become Christian, when in 303 A.D. the king of Armenia converted to Christianity. A large Armenian community arrived in the Holy City about a century after the conversion of their king, and when the kingdom itself vanished at the end of the fourth century, Jerusalem became the Armenian peoples' spiritual capital. They have had an unbroken presence here ever since, and thus the Armenian section remains one of the four major divisions in the Old City.

As we approach St. James, we enter through a gateway into a small courtyard with a fountain. At the entrance to the cathedral, a hooded monk is announcing the start of a religious service by striking two *synamids*, long wooden bars that produce the sound of gongs. Synamids have their origin in the Islamic occupation of Jerusalem during Ottoman times, when laws forbade the sound of church bells in the Holy City. Walking

inside the cathedral, illuminated by the flickering yellow light of countless hanging oil lamps, one is impressed by how richly it is decorated. The stone pavement floor is covered with thick oriental carpets, which, along with the many hanging lamps, provide a mystical peacefulness and a sense of the presence of the holy. To the left are two Patriarchal thrones, one inlaid with ivory and reverenced as the throne of Jerusalem's first bishop, James the Lesser, the cousin of Jesus, who is also commemorated at the cathedral. Close to the throne of the patriarch is a small chapel dedicated to Saint James the Lesser. In the pavement floor is implanted a small piece of red marble, indicating the spot revered as the site where he was beheaded in 65 A.D.

Reflection

While the focus of the Way of the Cross is upon the passion and death of Jesus, visiting this cathedral provides an opportunity to recall those brave disciples who faithfully took up their crosses and followed him. Being a loyal follower of Jesus of Galilee requires every baptized man and woman to carry with conviction the cross of conscience.

This cross of conscience mirrors the cross you embraced at your baptism, just as Jesus carried one under his wooden cross. To each person God has given a conscience by which to judge what is or is not God's will. It is your soul's Supreme Court, whose final decision supersedes all social, civil and religious laws. So sacred is this divine gift that we are bound to act out with conviction the decisions of our conscience.

Conviction means being of strong belief, but it also is related to being a convict, one convicted as guilty of an offense. The double implications of this word apply to those brave disciples of Christ whose deeply held beliefs have made them criminals. Because their conscience has contradicted prevailing civil or religious law, they were banished, imprisoned or executed. This site of the execution of the Apostle James silently shouts the question: Are you living your conscience with conviction, in such a way as to be subject to conviction?

Many of us lack conviction, being like tall reeds that sway whichever way the wind is blowing, needing to take a poll to find the will of the majority. Convictions based on conscience are truly crosses, for they can ostracize us from our circle of family, friends and associates. At this holy martyr's shrine, pray to the Spirit of God that you may prayerfully use your baptismal gift of freedom of conscience. Petition the Spirit for courage to embrace the cross of conscience with the fiery, impassioned conviction that is required of an authentic disciple of Christ. As a cross-carrying disciple whose personal Way of the Cross is down the main street of your world, ask yourself whether you are as committed as James the Decapitated or as prudent as Pontius Pilate.

This Armenian Cathedral is a shrine not only of Saint James; it symbolizes all those who have suffered — and suffer this day — because of embracing the cross of their conscience. This place on our pilgrimage could be called the Shrine-Tomb of the Unknown Martyrs. Look beneath these oriental carpets and see a maze of millions of red marble markers for those heroic casualties of the cross, regardless of which rite, sect or Christian denomination they espoused.

+

Let me take up my cross and follow you, Lord Jesus,
for by so doing I share in the liberation of the world.

THE SEVENTEENTH DAY OF THE PILGRIMAGE
Monday of the Third Week in Lent

THE SEVENTH STATION
PONTIUS PILATE CONDEMNS JESUS TO DEATH

We praise you and we follow you, O Christ,
because by our crosses united, we redeem the world.

Scripture for the Seventh Station

They bound Jesus, led him away and handed him over to Pilate.
Pilate questioned him, "Are you the king of the Jews?" He said to him
in reply, "You say so." The chief priests accused him of many things.
Again Pilate questioned him, "Have you no answer? See how many
things they accuse you of." Jesus gave him no further answer, so that
Pilate was amazed. —Mark 15: 1-5

Having returned to the Citadel of David (*see map on page 55*),
we are now in the *Omar ibn el-Khattab* Square, named for the

SEVENTH STATION — MONDAY OF THE THIRD WEEK • 99

first Muslim ruler of Jerusalem after the Arab conquest of A.D. 638. To the right as you face the fortress of the Citadel is a wide gap with a paved road, once part of a moat that was filled in and paved over. Before the moat was built here, it was the site of the broad stone platform of the Roman Praetorium onto which the Governor Pontius Pilate came to judge the Galilean Jesus.

Like the first trial, this second trial of Jesus of Nazareth is also a clash of kingdoms. Yesterday, when he stood before the Holy Sanhedrin, the kingdom of God present in the person of Jesus confronted the kingdom of religion. On the stone platform outside the Roman Praetorium, the kingdom of God contested with the powerful kingdom of Caesar.

To his credit, Pilate did not tolerate the false witnesses and nighttime secrecy of the religious courts, yet like all shrewd politicians he was swayed by the influence of the powerful religious elite and the whim of the populace. While Pilate may have been amazed by the courage and conviction of the prisoner Jesus, his astonishment was eclipsed by political expediency.

This seventh station is repeated countless times, whenever the peaceable kingdom of God encounters the powerful kingdoms of state and religion, especially when they are wed in a conspiracy of convenience and connivance. The casualty in these deadly confrontations of conscience and conviction is always God-in-human-flesh as revealed in Jesus of Nazareth. He affirmed that the reign of God is a peaceful kingdom, telling Pilate, "If my kingdom belonged to this world (of power and force), my attendants would be fighting to keep me from being handed over..." (John 18: 36). These last hours of Jesus' life were filled with false accusations, personal ridicule, insults and abuse, yet throughout it he enfleshed God's rejection of violence as a solution to any issue. In the abused humanity of the prisoner Jesus we see Divine Love invincibly unwavering before all the mighty powers of Rome and Religion.

Contemporary Reflection

The condemnation and crucifixion of Jesus were the result of violent political and religious conflicts in the Holy City of Jerusalem. Two thousand years later, those same conflicts continue to stain her streets with blood. As then, so today, those who come here on pilgrimage risk the loss of their lives to terrorists and the fanatic violence of religious fundamentalists. *(If you are interested in exploring this deadly aspect of the Holy City, a reflection on the endless river of blood that flows through Jerusalem can be found in this book's* Political Postlogue *on page 229.)*

Prayer for Quiet Conviction

Jesus, strong in silence before your judges,
    Jesus, secure in love's ultimate victory,
    Jesus, concerned only with God's judgment,
    I find hope in your courageous conviction.

Convince me of the divine reality
    that the innocent and weak are powerful,
    that when love and peace are our weapons,
    then truth and justice are invincible.

If the day comes when I must stand
    before the courts of the dark powers,
    falsely accused or a victim of rumor,
    let me possess your sure, quiet strength,
    your unshakable heroic conviction.

+

Let me take up my cross and follow you, Lord Jesus,
for by so doing I share in the liberation of the world.

SEVENTH STATION REFLECTION ON

Our Crosses United

We praise you and we follow you, O Christ,
because by our crosses united, we redeem the world.

Scripture for Shared Suffering

Now I rejoice in my sufferings for your sake, and in my flesh I am filling up what is lacking in the afflictions of Christ on behalf of his body, which is the church. —Colossians 1: 24

St. Paul was a convert, whose new life in Christ made him mystically aware of his intimate unity with the Risen Jesus and revealed to him how his personal sufferings were united with the redeeming mystery of the passion and death of Jesus. He spoke of the awareness of this potent communion of shared sufferings in his letter to the Philippians: "...to know him and the power of his resurrection and (the) sharing of his sufferings by being conformed to his death" (Philippians 3: 10). Writing to the Christians in Rome, he affirmed that the source of this Holy Communion is the cross: "...are you unaware that we who were baptized into Christ Jesus were baptized into his death? (Romans 6: 3).

Paul's question is a Lenten examination that asks if we are aware that, fundamentally, we were baptized not into some church but into the cross of Calvary. He further asks us to reflect on what it means to be plunged into the cross, sufferings and death of Jesus. This book's version of the Stations of the Cross is based on the union of the baptism of Jesus in the Jordan with our personal baptisms. Paul asks, "Are you aware?" Are you aware that by a mystical communion of crosses your physical and emotional sufferings are one with those of Christ? The next time you suffer the pains of arthritis, or a migraine

BY OUR CROSSES UNITED, WE REDEEM THE WORLD

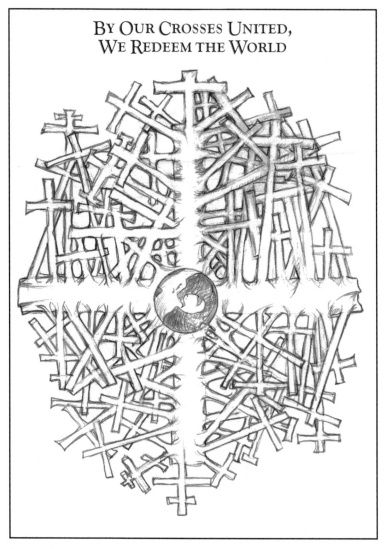

headache or some social rejection, use your faith awareness to call down the Holy Spirit to deepen your awareness of that mystical union so you can consciously consecrate your pain into the living passion of Jesus.

To walk the Way of the Cross is not to engage in pious pretending, to step back in history and reenact a passion play.

Authentically walking the Way of the Cross is not playacting; it is the daily performance of your disciple's duty. The Way of the Cross is the saving road that leads up from the Jordan baptism to the dead end on Calvary, which then surprisingly breaks open onto the Alleluia Avenue of Easter.

Paradoxically, it is here at Pilate's Praetorium that you are to enter into a marriage. With great affection you are to marry your cross to the cross of Jesus right at this place where he is about to take up his cross and drag it to his death on Calvary. A wedding is a union of lovers; so you are invited to climb up into the nuptial bed of Christ's cross. There, as he is crucified, his life and your life together are consummated. The pilgrimage of baptism leads to a living crucifixion, as Paul said, "I have been crucified with Christ; yet I live, no longer I, but Christ lives in me" (Galatians 2: 19-20).

Prayer for Wedding Crosses

Fire of the Holy Spirit, be a raging forge
in which my Savior's cross and mine
are fused together forever as one,
a holy wedding of our pains and agonies.

Without whining or complaining,
I lovingly and freely open myself
to be pierced by the hideous nails
of my pains, aches and sufferings,
to be crucified with my Beloved.

+

*Let me take up my cross and follow you, Lord Jesus,
for by so doing I share in the liberation of the world.*

Tuesday of the Third Week in Lent

THE EIGHTH STATION

JESUS IS SCOURGED
AND CROWNED WITH THORNS

We praise you and we follow you, O Christ,
because by our crosses united, we redeem the world.

Scripture for the Eighth Station

Then Pilate took Jesus and had him scourged. The soldiers wove a
crown out of thorns and placed it on his head, and clothed him in a
purple cloak, and they came to him and said, "Hail, King of the
Jews!" And they struck him repeatedly." –John 19: 1-3

Scourging was a public spectacle and, like crucifixion, was a public
punishment. The flogging of a prisoner could be done either
lightly with elm branch switches or brutally with leather straps

tipped with pieces of lead or bone. The latter form was likely the one used on Jesus, because Pilate was attempting to make him an object of pity so he would be spared of having to die on the cross. After his scourging, the mockery of the soldiers began.

A mock crown of thorns was jammed upon Jesus' head. Rome's Caesars wore a green laurel-leaf-wreath as a crown, symbolic of their military victories. Nike, the Greek goddess of victory, had crowned her victors with laurel wreaths, and the Romans adopted this mythic practice as a sign of their triumphant spirit and of the "Peace of Rome" that followed the defeat of their enemies. Laurel leaves were also sacred to the god Apollo and were believed to cleanse souls of their guilt, especially the souls of those who had shed blood. Thus, it was highly symbolic when the soldiers made a wreath of twisted gray branches with piercing thorns and mockingly crowned their Prisoner, who was the Pardoner of the guilt of others.

Of course, the crown of thorns the soldiers imbedded into Jesus' head was intended to be a sign of his defeat and not his victory. Yet it also echoes back to the burning bush out of which God spoke to Moses, for that bush was believed to be a desert thornbush. Out of its flames God called Moses to liberate the Hebrews from their slavery. We might wonder if Jesus heard God speaking out of the flaming penetration of his thorns, "I will not abandon you, my precious beloved — free my people," enabling him to endure the searing pain of the sharp thorns that pieced his head. Was Jesus' ability to embrace his suffering with silent composure based on his conviction that just as Moses' thornbush was not consumed by fire, he would not be consumed by his fiery passion?

At this Eighth Station, prayerfully ponder whether in baptism every true follower is given a wreath of defeat, a garland of grief, along with a cross. As you sit in silent prayer, weave your wreath of thorns out of your troubled thoughts, painful memories and fearful anxieties about the future — a crown you can invisibly wear as a companion to your cross. Wear your hidden garland proudly so you may share the wreath of victory with Christ the Victor. For by your conscious sharing in his painful passion and death, you also share in his glorious resurrection, in his victorious liberation and redemption of the world.

In a unique way, those disciples who suffer from emotional and psychological problems or mental illnesses are crowned in communion with their Beloved. Even headaches can be redemptive when they are united to his thorny headband of heartache, agony and anguish.

Station Prayer of My Crown of Thorns

Fingers of the Spirit, weave a wreath
    out of my troubled thoughts and anxieties
    like the one Jesus wore to his death.
Whenever affliction throbs in my head
    and I am pierced by the sharp thorns
    of painful regret, grief and failure,
    may I slowly make the sign of the cross
    upon my invisibly wreathed forehead.

This tracing of the cross renews the one
    drawn upon my forehead in baptism,
    when I was sealed in Christ's death
    and in the victory of his resurrection.
O Fiery Spirit of God, my precious baptismal gift,
    consecrate my agonies into a sacrifice,
    transforming my afflictions of body, mind and soul
    into the loving redemption of the world.

+

*Let me take up my cross and follow you, Lord Jesus,
for by so doing I share in the liberation of the world.*

THE NINETEENTH DAY OF THE PILGRIMAGE

Wednesday of the Third Week in Lent

THE MOCKERY OF THE KING'S GAME

We praise you and we follow you, O Christ,
because by our crosses united, we redeem the world.

The Roman soldiers played a game with Jesus called *Basilinda*,
"King." In the game, knucklebones were often used as tokens to
be tossed like dice. The winner of this game of chance could
select a victim to play the role of king. This person was chosen
from among the prisoners awaiting execution, and the soldiers
would crown him and appropriately invest him in a robe. Then
they would mockingly salute him as they would a real Caesar.
The Roman soldiers used whatever accessories they could find:
The cloak might be a tattered red army blanket, and the crown
would be made from the branches of any pliable plant. In the
case of Jesus, the crown was likely woven out of a common weed-
like plant in the area of Jerusalem that had small, sharp thorns.

Basilinda started as a barrack-room diversion to relieve
military boredom. The King Game was also an outlet for lowly
soldiers to mock their superiors, whom they were bound to obey
under the pain of death. The soldiers loved some generals and
governors, and they despised others. By mocking, taunting and
teasing their royal-robed prisoners, they could release any pent-
up frustration and resentment without fear of reprisals from
their superiors.

The teasing of others is usually dismissed as simply a form
of innocent kidding. Yet it is often no less innocent of malice
than the teasing and taunting of Jesus was harmless play. Such
teasing is an act of violence, whose weapons are words that

pierce their victims by making fun of them. The ancient Roman game of Basilinda is still a favorite sport of school playgrounds, and those who have ever had to endure it know how Jesus must have felt. Some who have found no other outlet for their feelings of inferiority never graduate from this evil childhood play. In an attempt to disguise their poverty of self-esteem, even as adults they become ridiculers by using cruel jokes and slurs to mock those of other races or ethic backgrounds and those with different sexual or religious orientations.

Whenever you are belittled and forced to bear a thorny crown of ridicule and sarcasm, give thanks for this opportunity to share in the redeeming passion of Christ. The prisoner Jesus did not stand up for his rights; he humbly sat in shame, robbed of his dignity while being robed as a mock king. Jesus did not cry out but was silent; so the next time you must painfully experience teasing disguised as good-natured fun, do so in his pattern. Embrace it not with stoic silence, but rather with joyful gratitude that you have been found worthy to have a share in God's work of redemption.

And if you should ever be tempted to tease another, remember the mocking of Jesus. You might envision yourself dressed in the garb of a Roman soldier, like the cohort here at Pilate's Praetorium, and exchange the person you are tempted to tease with Jesus of Galilee. Then, if possible, have fun playing the ancient game of mockery.

+

Let me take up my cross and follow you, Lord Jesus,
for by so doing I share in the liberation of the world.

Thursday of the Third Week in Lent

THE NINTH STATION
JESUS IS MOCKED AND GIVEN HIS CROSS

We praise you and we follow you, O Christ,
because by our crosses united, we redeem the world.

Scripture for the Ninth Station

The soldiers led him away inside the palace, that is, the praetorium,
and assembled the whole cohort.... They began to salute him...and
kept striking his head with a reed and spitting upon him. They knelt
before him in homage. And when they had mocked him, they stripped
him of the purple cloak, dressed him in his own clothes, and led him
out to crucify him. —Mark 15: 16, 18-20

Some thirty years before the trial of Jesus, the Magi, guided by
a star, came to this very palace of Herod. These foreigners

inquired about where they might find "the newborn king of the Jews," so they could pay him homage with gold, frankincense and myrrh. On this Sad Friday at the very same site, another group of foreigners paid homage to the "King of the Jews" born in Bethlehem — but now with slaps, spittle and sneers.

At this station Jesus is crucified with mockery, a crucifixion of shame that entailed a dying to his dignity that is as painful as any physical death. As the spittle of the soldiers dribbled down his face, no doubt his own words from the Sermon on the Mount must have echoed in his heart, "Blessed are you when they insult you and persecute you and utter every kind of evil against you falsely because of me. Rejoice and be glad, for your reward will be great in heaven" (Matthew 5: 11-12). When Jesus said, "because of *me*," the me of which he spoke included his beloved God with whom he was united, and who had inspired his words about the divine reward. Jesus' complete identification with his God made the persecution of one into a rejection of both.

To be able to rejoice in the midst of great physical or emotional suffering is never easy and, in fact, may be impossible. As a Roman plaything, the prisoner Jesus wasn't smiling when they slapped and insulted him, but, by living what he taught, he must have found solace in his suffering and moved closer to the source of true joy. Solace means comfort, or cheer, and it is possible to find a real comfort in one's pain when it has meaning and purpose for oneself and others. A mother, for example, experiences solace in the midst of the intense pain of giving birth because of the knowledge that her suffering is bringing her precious child into the world.

The Spirit spurred Jesus at his Last Supper to anticipate his shame and pain, inspiring him to embrace his suffering and place it at the service of others. "This is my blood — my pain — which will be shed for you and for all," he told his friends around that table. By this dedication, Jesus' passion and death became a sacrifice — from the Latin *sacer facere*,

JESUS CONSECRATING HIS CROSS

meaning "to make sacred." The reality of suffering and death, which is universally shared by all creatures and all of creation, was made sacred for all time by his consecration.

"Do this in memory of me" is a discipleship invitation for you to dedicate and donate your pain and suffering for others. Pain imprisons you in solitary confinement. Making your suffering a loving gift, while you are still submerged in it, is one of the most difficult acts of self-denial and self-forgetfulness. Yet when you are able to let your physical pain be such a gift, you can experience an exodus from your suffering because it now has real meaning and purpose. Jesus said we were to follow him, and we most closely walk in his way when we enact this sacred Eucharist of consecrating our pain and suffering.

Jesus' response to his passion and torture was not that of a stoic; rather, his silence was saturated with the solace of God's Spirit. This same solace is available to all his cross-carrying disciples. In your personal suffering, pray for the solace of the Spirit, and then heroically give away your suffering for the good of those you love and for the healing of unknown others. Pain is energy, and when consecrated by the Spirit it becomes a positive, enriching energy for the redemption of the world. When next you are visited by pain, remember that your baptismal anointing as a priestly person of God empowers you to celebrate the Mass of Suffering.

Prayer for the Consecration of Suffering

O Spirit of Solace, Comforter of God,
    bandage me within your healing anointing
    each time I am in pain and adversity.
O Sacrificial Spirit of Love,
    who inspired Jesus at his Last Supper
    to pour out as gift his painful agony,
    inspire me to do the same with my suffering.

Whenever I stand at pain's threshold,
    remind me to dedicate my sorrows
    as my personal legacy and gift of love
    for those I love and for all peoples.
By such frequent consecrations of pain,
    may I prayerfully prepare for the day
    when at last I am bedbound for death.

+

Let me take up my cross and follow you, Lord Jesus,
for by so doing I share in the liberation of the world.

The Twenty-First Day of the Pilgrimage
Friday of the Third Week in Lent

Meditation on the Way of the Cross Through Jerusalem's David Street

We praise you and we follow you, O Christ,
because by our crosses united, we redeem the world.

Scripture for the Way of the Cross
...(They) led him out to crucify him. —Mark 15: 20

These seven short words from Mark contain the absolute horror and agony of Jesus' journey from Pilate's Praetorium to the Mount of Calvary. As our pilgrimage now departs from the Citadel at the Jaffa Gate and moves down David Street (*see map on page 118*), take up your cross as a faithful disciple and follow the way along which Jesus carried his cross to his death. Convicted criminals were forced to carry their own instruments of death, the cross beams that would be attached to the main shaft of their crosses. This street we walk is named after King David, just as the Citadel is known as the Tower of David. Set on an east-west axis of the city, as the Romans rebuilt it in A.D. 135, David Street terminates at the Temple Mount.

More a narrow alleyway than a street, it winds through the markets of the Old City crowded with tourists, pilgrims, pushcarts and pushy merchants. The stone street is actually a series of short broad steps, so watch where you step, as you can be easily distracted by merchants on both sides trying to attract you into their shops. Watch not only your step; also watch your wallet or purse, since any street crowded with tourists, pilgrims and shoppers also has its share of pickpockets and thieves. Moreover,

Shops along an Old City Souq (Alleyway)

the merchants loudly hawk all sorts of products — from food, dresses and leather goods to holy souvenirs — and sell them by the old system of haggling with customers. In this ancient art of bargaining, the usual gauge for the customer is to haggle down the price to at least two thirds of what the shopkeeper is asking.

Unlike the pious scenes we usually envision in the Stations of the Cross, it was down just such a narrow, dirty, garbage-littered street filled with haggling merchants that Jesus of Galilee struggled to carry his cross, unable to watch his steps. Upon reaching *Khan al-Zeit* Street, we turn to our left and travel north up this way that leads through the Butcher's Market. The slaughtered lambs and animal carcasses that hang from hooks remind us of the Lamb of God, the flogged slave of God, who was led on this very route through the crowds to Golgotha.

How fitting that the Way of the Cross is forced to make its way through an ancient shopping center! In a way, Christianity has become a Merchant's Way of the Cross, where each sect and denomination haggle to attract potential convert-customers to enter their pious shop and purchase a membership in their religion. The shops along this street are filled with cheap trinkets and with costly souvenirs of the Holy City: rosaries, paintings, religious medals, crosses in all sizes, and stacks of bibles. May this shoddy commercial reality remind you of how often the way of life Jesus lived has been turned into a religion that sells Jesus. May your traveling the Way of the Cross place upon your shoulders like a crossbeam the critical question of this pilgrimage: Is your religion one that is *about* Jesus, or is it one of following the Way of Jesus?

The real religion of Jesus remains as revolutionary today as it was two thousand years ago. He clearly said there was no need for elaborate temples or churches, or for their sacred priesthoods and clergy. The Way of Jesus called his disciples to embrace nonviolence and nonjudgment, to practice constant forgiving and to refrain from condemning others or returning injury for injury. A good Lenten examination of conscience would be a slow and careful reading of the requirements for belonging to the religion of Jesus found in Matthew's Gospel, chapters five through seven. Jesus must have known that the majority could only be members of a religion *about* him, for near the end of his Sermon of the Mount, he says, "Enter through the narrow gate...how narrow the road that leads to life. And those who find it are few" (Matthew 7: 13-14).

The challenge of every Christian, every disciple, is to belong to the religion of the few by following Jesus' narrow way that leads to life. If this has not been your way, know it is never too late to change your direction. So, pilgrim to the Holy City, beware of the pickpockets of the soul found on religion's crowded streets. Stay clear of those spiritual merchants eager to haggle down the price of discipleship.

+

Let me take up my cross and follow you, Lord Jesus,
for by so doing I share in the liberation of the world.

THE TWENTY-SECOND DAY OF THE PILGRIMAGE
Saturday of the Third Week in Lent

REFLECTION ON THE VIA DOLOROSA

We praise you and we follow you, O Christ,
because by our crosses united, we redeem the world.

The Via Dolorosa, the Way of Sorrow, the traditional Way of the Cross walked by pilgrims, begins and winds its way through the Moslem Quarter of the Holy City. It is more a walk of faith and devotion than a retracing of Jesus' steps or taking the actual route followed by the first Christian pilgrims. On Holy Thursday night, for example, Byzantine Eastern Catholics would walk in procession from Gethsemane to the site of Calvary. Then in the Middle Ages, the Latin, or Roman, rite Catholics created the present path of the Way of the Cross, with the Fourteenth Station, the Burial of Jesus, located in the Church of the Holy Sepulcher. Again, the present Way of the Cross begins on the opposite or eastern side of the city, where at one time the Roman Fortress Antonia stood. The convent of the Sisters of Zion now occupies this site of the first and second stations of the Via Dolorosa. The lower level of the convent contains shrine markers to what was believed in the Middle Ages to be the location of Pilate's Praetorium, where Jesus was scourged, condemned and given his crossbeam to carry.

The Gospel of Matthew, however, refers to Jesus' trial as taking place on a stone platform (Matthew 27: 19), like the one known to have existed at King Herod's palace. Moreover, Luke's Gospel states that his trial was conducted outside in the open (Luke 23: 4). These texts support the premise of contemporary scholars that Pilate's judgment site was located at the Citadel on the other side of the city. While our Pilgrimage of the Cross and

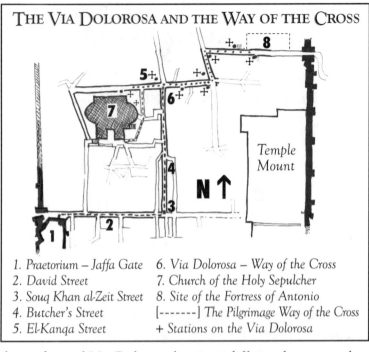

THE VIA DOLOROSA AND THE WAY OF THE CROSS

Temple Mount

N ↑

1. Praetorium – Jaffa Gate
2. David Street
3. Souq Khan al-Zeit Street
4. Butcher's Street
5. El-Kanqa Street
6. Via Dolorosa – Way of the Cross
7. Church of the Holy Sepulcher
8. Site of the Fortress of Antonio
[-------] The Pilgrimage Way of the Cross
+ Stations on the Via Dolorosa

the traditional Via Dolorosa began at different locations, they will converge at the site of what was once the city gate, *Porta Judicaria*, that led out of Jerusalem to the hill of Golgotha.

An Artist's Lesson on Cross Carrying

Which street, road or alley Jesus actually walked carrying his cross is not terribly significant. What is much more essential is how he carried his cross, the grace with which he painfully hauled the apparatus of his death. More than simply dragging it, he demonstrated the *art* of carrying one's cross. As we stop to pray at the following stations, be aware of his graceful skill in this difficult and unique art. Jesus the carpenter applied the artistry of his lifelong craftsmanship to his final masterpiece of wood. Like you and me, he was made in the image of God, and as *the* Divine Image he mirrored God in the flesh without ugly distortions of selfishness or greed or the appetite to exercise power over others. God's image was reflected back with crystal clarity in the Holy Carpenter because he conscientiously planed away and sanded off his human imperfections. While we have been religiously influenced to see the power and compassion of God sublimely revealed in the miracles of Jesus, it is actually here in his artistry of carrying his cross that we see the most authentic and transparent reflection of the love and power of God.

Each of us has been made by the imagination of God, and each of us has a share in that divine imagination. With that gift we are to creatively carry our crosses in life. The master artist Jesus transformed his cross of barren wood into the fruit tree of life for all the world. We are called to follow him and become skilled in the art of suffering, for every cross is invested with cosmic potential. How each of us transforms our cross has divine implications beyond our wildest dreams, since God desires that they are to have an influence upon all of creation. All crosses, visible and invisible, are intended to be tools of transformation for those to whom they are given and for the whole cosmos.

The next stations we will visit are art studios in which the Beloved of God transformed his burden of disgrace into the most glorious grace by being gracefully absentminded of himself and his heavy cross. On this his execution route he ignored his own excruciating pain to practice the art of showing compassion toward those he encountered. In the process he failed to be a strong person! He fell again and again under the burden of his cross, and yet each time he artfully rose up from these failures to begin his work again. In a poverty of passion, he graciously and generously allowed another to take up his burden and carry it for him. Let us learn from this master of suffering the great art of how to share our pains and crosses, an action more heroic than hoarding them in an ego-inflating feat of strength.

+

Let me take up my cross and follow you, Lord Jesus,
for by so doing I share in the liberation of the world.

The Fourth Sunday of the Pilgrimage
Laetare, Joyful, Sunday

We praise you and we follow you, O Christ,
because by our crosses united, we redeem the world.

This Sunday is the middle point in our pilgrimage through the Lenten Season. It was named after the opening words in the old Latin Mass text: *Laetare Jerusalem,* "Rejoice, O Jerusalem." This Sunday once was a single joyful note sounded in the middle of the forty long, gloomy penitential days of Lent. The traditional Way of the Cross is usually a somber, mournful march along the way of sorrow. This Joyful Sunday, however, raises the question: Should it be?

It seems that the fourteenth century Italian Franciscans named the Via Dolorosa after the Italian musical term *dolorosa,* meaning "to play with sadness." The traditional devotion of the Way of the Cross is a sad, sorrowful journey of the death of Jesus of Galilee. Yet unless it truly dead-ends with the death and burial of Jesus, is it appropriate that the way of the redemption should be a Sad Way? When this devotion ends with Jesus' burial in the tomb, then it truly is a mournful procession, like following the coffin of a loved one to the grave. The Via Dolorosa is also the appropriate name for any spirituality or theology that focuses upon our personal sinful responsibility for the death of Jesus on his cross and the resulting necessity of continuous penitence and remorse.

This Pilgrimage Way of the Cross does not dead-end at the tomb of Jesus but will move beyond that "final" Fourteenth Station and the darkness of Good Friday into the sunrise glory of Easter — and beyond! The Latin *via* means "way," and with a proper understanding of Christ's death and resurrection, the Way of the Cross becomes the *Via Gaudioso,* an exultant, joyful way. Like *dolorosa*, the term *gaudioso* is an Italian musical term; it indicates that a melody is to be played "with joy and gladness." To travel the route of the passion with joy requires remembering that after we ascend the ugly hill of Jesus' crucifixion and death, the way leads beyond his tomb to his resurrection on Easter. Our Via Gaudioso will also lead beyond Easter to the glorious stations of his triumphant cross: the appearances of the Risen Jesus to his disciples, his gifting them with the Holy Spirit, and finally his ascension and commissioning of them to go forth to proclaim the good news.

Who of us walks a Via Dolorosa on our way to a wedding? This Pilgrimage Way of the Cross is a wedding march to the marriage of heaven with earth, of humanity with God, of pain with joy and death with life. The reason we can rejoice in this seeming tragedy resides in God's victory over death revealed in the raising up of the dead Jesus. Our joy flows from the fact that this journey is a prototype procession of our personal life journey, in which death is destroyed by Life. We can walk this road of the cross with joy because by his death and rising, Christ destroyed death and transformed our crosses into holy ladders by which we also climb into the heart of God.

Walk this Via Alleluia with the same bittersweet bliss as you would walk in funeral processions carrying a loved one to the grave. While missing your beloved's physical presence, laughter, affection and companionship — for a while — our faith convinces us that our painful loss gives way to joyful glory. "Be always joyful, pray continually and give thanks whatever happens" (1 Thessalonians 5: 16-18). Come, fellow pilgrims, let us return to the Via Gaudioso, the Alleluia Way.

+

Let me take up my cross and follow you, Lord Jesus,
for by so doing I share in the liberation of the world.

"*Even now, I find my joy in the suffering I endure for you. In my own flesh I fill up what is lacking in the sufferings of Christ*" —*Colossians 1: 24*

FIND YOUR JOY IN YOUR SUFFERING

To find joy in your personal suffering, it helps to remember the words of Paul of Tarsus: "Even now, I find my joy in the suffering I endure for you. In my own flesh I fill up what is lacking in the sufferings of Christ" (Colossians 1: 24). Paul also spoke about a most unique Way of the Cross, in which the cross is within our flesh. Indeed, it is the way of our common Calvary, the place where we share in the dying of Jesus. In his letter to the Corinthians he expanded on this communion of affliction: "We are afflicted in every way (*consider the multitude of pains contained in his word "every"*)...always carrying about in our body the dying of Jesus.... For we who live are constantly being taken up to death for the sake of Jesus, so that the life of Jesus may be manifested in our mortal flesh" (2 Corinthians 4: 8, 10-11).

When we are visited by suffering in any form, we experience the evaporation of the illusion that we possess any real control over our lives, and this awareness adds to our pain. Yet when we embrace as the cross of our human condition the reality that we, along with all creation, must suffer in this life — and then unite our suffering to the passion of Christ — then we can find true joy. This joy comes from becoming a living Calvary, a living sacrifice that mysteriously allows us to share in the life of Christ and even, in an inexplicable way, to supply "what is lacking in the sufferings of Christ." In his *Angel in Armor* Ernest Becker wrote, "Sadness is a sin in Judeo-Christian thought because it reflects a lack of faith in God's design."

Monday of the Fourth Week in Lent

THE TENTH STATION

SIMON OF CYRENE HELPS JESUS CARRY HIS CROSS

We praise you and we follow you, O Christ,
because by our crosses united, we redeem the world.

Scripture for the Twenty-Third Day

They pressed into service a passerby, Simon, a Cyrenian, who was coming in from the country, the father of Alexander and Rufus, to carry his cross. —Mark 15: 21

Mark, Matthew and Luke all name for posterity the bystander in the crowd whom the Roman soldiers commandeered to help Jesus carry his cross. The fact that the gospel writers appear to know who he was suggests that Simon was likely a disciple.

Cyrenaica was a North African Roman province along the coast of the Mediterranean, and Cyrene was its capital. The city was known for its large population of Greek-speaking Jews, and so it is possible that Simon may have come to Jerusalem as a Passover pilgrim.

Roman execution law dictated that a condemned prisoner must carry his own cross. The act of commandeering someone from the crowd to carry the Prisoner's heavy cross implies that the soldiers were afraid Jesus might die before they could crucify him. It's likely they feared he was so weakened by his scourging that he wouldn't make it to Golgotha.

The narrow street was jammed with pilgrims, spectators, shoppers and the curious drawn to the entertainment of a public execution. Perhaps along with Simon of Cyrene there were other disciples of Jesus anonymously present in that mob. But apparently none was willing to reach out and shoulder the Master's burden. Was Simon of Cyrene drafted against his will and forced to leave the security of the crowd to assist Jesus in taking up his cross? Or was being drafted for this unseemly task an answer to his prayers to God for Jesus? If so, fate had given him the unique gift to assist his suffering Master.

A disciple is someone magnetically drawn to a gifted person. More than a fan, a disciple's fascination is to imitate, to become a student and follower of an intriguing teacher. The charismatic teacher from Galilee, with his all-embracing, unconditional love and captivating presence, attracted large, enthusiastic crowds and many disciples. Some disciples were so drawn to him as to leave their usual responsibilities of family and follow him as he traveled throughout the land speaking about God's love and announcing the new reign of God.

On the other hand, there is nothing one might find magnetically attractive about a scourged, bleeding, thorn-crowned, ridiculed Jesus stumbling to his death along this crowded, narrow street. Disciples are not usually drawn to cripples. People are not often magnetically drawn to prisoners condemned to death. Those who live on death row have few disciples eager to follow them. Winners draw admirers and imitators; losers walk alone. Discipleship is more than simply association with a master; it is an imitate identification. On that fateful Friday, however, of those who once prided themselves as being Jesus' intimate disciples, none dared even to associate publicly with him as a follower.

This Tenth Station challenges us with several increasingly difficult questions: Am I a disciple of the gentle Jesus, the loving teacher who healed the sick and lame and whom children gathered around, wanting to sit in his lap?

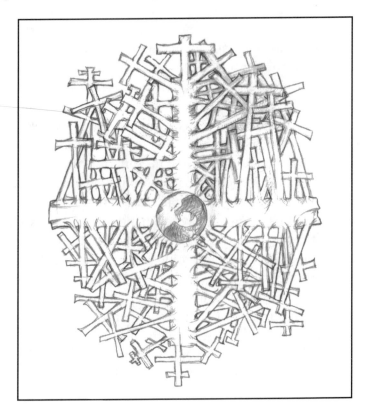

Am I a faithful disciple of that Jesus who became an outcast in the eyes of the religiously respectable and pious because he excluded no one — even sinners and foreigners — from being his friend and thus was guilty of sin by association?

Am I a disciple who is not ashamed of the naked, disgraced and crucified Jesus?

Do I gladly seize the opportunity, as did Simon of Cyrene, to carry the cross of the suffering Christ present in another person, especially one who is rejected by the crowd?

Prayer of Carrying Crosses

The road of life is crowded
   with those carrying crosses —
   those who have been flogged and abused
   by old age, poverty or alcohol,
   by a poor education, drugs or crime.

When I see them pass my way,
   do I hide — playing a spectator —
   or do I freely step forward
   to lift up their cross,
   adding it to mine,
   as did Simon of Cyrene?

+

Let me take up my cross, and that of others,
and follow you, Lord Jesus,
for by so doing I share in the liberation of the world.

Jesus Falls with His Cross

Stations Three, Seven and Nine in the traditional Way of the Cross are dedicated to Jesus falling with his cross. None of these falls are recorded in the gospel passion accounts. However, as we saw in our Tenth Station, the fact that the Roman soldiers commandeered Simon of Cyrene to help Jesus carry his cross strongly suggests that our Savior struggled under the weight of his cross.

Every disciple has experienced falling beneath the burden of his or her cross. Rather than judging these failures as a lack of physical strength, emotional determination or the capacity to love, like Jesus, we usually fall simply because of the weight of our crosses. Some devotions of the cross invite us to meditate on how the weight of our personal sins caused Jesus to collapse with his cross and that we, therefore, are to blame for his painful falls. You might, instead, consider Jesus' failure to shoulder his cross effortlessly over the entire distance to Calvary as a holy invitation to show yourself compassion for the times when you have fallen under your cross. Rather than occasions of impatience, irritation, feeling sorry for yourself or even resentment for having a cross to bear, our falls can be blessings. Being compassionate with yourself gives birth to the courage to stand up again, shoulder your cross and continue on your personal way of the cross.

The laughter, jeers and ridicule must have showered down upon Jesus like acid rain as he stumbled and fell face down into the garbage-littered street. The few women weeping at the sight of the passion-soaked prophet stumbling past them were a tiny minority in the crowd that lined the way to Calvary. As we witness so often today, the majority are delighted to see someone held in high regard fall and become a scapegoat of shame and ridicule. Cultivating compassion under the weight of our crosses will prevent us from secretly delighting in the shame of famous and important people — as well as friends — who fall from grace. Such compassion will remove us from the crowd that laughingly jeered at Jesus underneath his cross, face down in the filth of the Via Dolorosa.

Tuesday of the Fourth Week in Lent

A MEDITATION ON THE MERGING OF THE VIA DOLOROSA AND THE VIA GAUDIOSO

We praise you and we follow you, O Christ,
for by our crosses united, we redeem the world.

Our pilgrimage route of the Via Gaudioso will soon merge with the Via Dolorosa when *El Khanqa* Street intersects *Souq Khan al-Zeit* Street *(see map on page 118)*. A *souq* is a Middle Eastern bazaar located in a crowded alleyway world of small shops full of brilliant colors, open displays of exotic foods — with meats, fruits and rich pastries — and vibrantly alive with all kinds of sounds and pungent aromas. As we go deeper into the souq, the natural light dims because of its arched vaulted ceiling, which only heightens the voices of pestering merchants and the sounds of the noisy crowds of people. Hidden from our eyes and beneath our feet is the memory-soaked pavement of the ancient Roman street down which Jesus painfully stumbled behind Simon of Cyrene, who now was carrying the Master's cross.

Today's Old City souq-market, with its narrow alley-like streets, has remained unchanged for many centuries. As you squeeze your way through the living river of surging, shoving people, you can visualize that it was through just such a bustling marketplace that Jesus and the other two condemned criminals were led. His way of the cross was jammed with spectators and curious onlookers fascinated by the sight of blood and brutality. Violence and evil have a certain magnetic lure — that is, as long as the violence is happening to someone else. Murder and brutality make headline stories in newspapers and primetime

A Quiet Section of the Via Dolorosa

television news — and the more bloody and brutal a situation, the more exposure it is given. Today's media spectators share the primal fascination with violence seen in those unsympathetic, gaping viewers in the souq who were eyewitnesses to the brutal punishment being inflicted on Jesus. Perhaps that primitive hunger for blood and brutality explains our seeming preference for a thorn-crowned, bleeding, crucified Jesus over an image of the gloriously victorious and radiantly beautiful Risen Christ. Perhaps that same desire helps explain our apparent partiality for Christian penance and mortification instead of gospel joy and delight.

In Lent it is customary for Christians to practice various personal mortifications. The Latin word *mortificare* means to cause to die, and these voluntary acts of penance and self-discipline seek to deaden the flesh by denying valid bodily appetites and desires. Discipline is essential to being a disciple and is necessary in any good spirituality. Moreover, mortification is a positive exercise when it is truly mortifying. The latter is a medical term that refers to the dying of a part of the human body, as when it is infected with gangrene. For the disciple, what needs to die is the little ego, the part of the self obsessed only with its own needs. As the Master said, "Take up your cross and deny your very self" (Matthew 16: 24).

Such physical acts of self-denial as fasting are certainly challenging, if only because of our primal need for food. Our primitive ancestors, not knowing if they would find any food for days, would gorge themselves on whatever was a hand. Indeed, all of our bodily appetites are prehistorically programmed to guard, promote and protect the self. Because mortifying the flesh has a long history as a way of strengthening one's spiritual resolve, and because such discipline is so contrary to our conditioning, it would be natural to take pride in these spiritual accomplishments. Therein lies the danger of this kind of penance, for our spiritual "bodybuilding" can easily inflate rather than shrink the ego.

Wholesome penance is found by imitating Jesus on that first Good Friday. Each disciple bears a cross — or crosses — that lead to a healthy penitential dying to self. Moreover, each day of our lives provides excellent opportunities for mortification: sitting calmly without anger in the midst of stalled traffic; waiting with a peaceful heart in a long, slow-moving checkout line, setting aside our personal preferences or desire for self-gratification in order to promote life and growth in a spouse, child, friend or even a stranger. The self dies small deaths whenever we embrace the physical aches and the emotional struggles presented to us in our family, work and other life experiences.

The paradox of penance as a pilgrim of the Way can be found in the newly adopted name of our pilgrimage, the Via Gaudioso. Consider exercising the truly difficult penances of daily abstaining from sadness and cynicism, of fasting from presumption and complacency. Most importantly, in the midst of these penances, practice rejoicing always, which St. Paul tells us is the will of God. "Rejoice always. Pray without ceasing. In all circumstances give thanks, for this is the will of God for you in Christ Jesus" (1 Thessalonians 5: 16-18). So, instead of taking upon yourself some self-chosen painful penance, with joy-soaked gratitude daily embrace your personal cross as an instrument for the redemptive healing of the world.

Rooted in an attitude of joy, we return now to our pilgrimage and move on to the Eleventh Station of the Cross. Be aware that deep beneath the pavement of this souq market-street was the ancient road that led to what once was Jerusalem's Old City gate that opened out to the hill of Calvary. Be aware, too, that as Jesus traveled this Via Dolorosa, deep beneath his sorrow and suffering was a ground of great joy that came from doing God's will.

+

Let me take up my cross and follow you, Lord Jesus,
for by so doing I share in the liberation of the world.

Wednesday of the Fourth Week in Lent

THE ELEVENTH STATION
JESUS MEETS THE WOMEN OF JERUSALEM

We praise you and we follow you, O Christ,
because by our crosses united, we redeem the world.

Scripture for the Eleventh Station

A large crowd of people followed Jesus, including many women who mourned and lamented him. Jesus turned to them and said, "Daughters of Jerusalem, do not weep for me; weep instead for yourselves and your children." —Luke 23: 27-28

Not all of those who crowded that narrow market street were hungry for blood and brutality. There were also women present who openly lamented the painful suffering of Jesus. When he turned to speak to them, did he see among them certain women whom he knew and loved? Did the group of weeping women contain his dear friends Mary and Martha of Bethany, or the adulterous woman he had saved from stoning, or the woman at the well whom he released and empowered? Was their mourning presence a solace to him, an expression of the consoling presence of his much-beloved Father? The prophet Isaiah spoke of such divine solace: "God says...like a son comforted by his mother will I comfort you" (Isaiah 66: 12).

As we join our crosses to Christ's on this pilgrimage way, God comforts you and me in our sufferings just as God comforted Jesus in his agony through the presence of those who are compassionate to us. Unlike pity, experiencing true sorrow for someone who is suffering is a form of compassionate communion with that person's sickness or pain. Moreover, at this station Jesus models for us the ultimate expression of compassion: being compassionate toward those who are mourning for you, who are suffering because of your distress. Forgetting the burden of your own cross as you give solace to others who are being crushed by their crosses is to live out the example and the appeal of Jesus to "be compassionate as your Creator in heaven is compassionate" (Luke 6: 36). As the medieval German mystic Meister Eckhart said, the best name for God is Compassion. So when you show compassion to another, you provide that person with a mystical experience, a revelation of God.

It seems that just before the scene of this Eleventh Station the soldiers released Simon of Cyrene from his obligation and sent him on his way. After they again roughly jammed the heavy crossbeam down on the shoulders of Jesus, he was again on his Way. As he struggled to straighten up under the load of his cross, he could see the city gate up ahead. He knew that beyond it was the hill of Golgotha, "the Skull," the place of Roman executions. As he braced himself for the great torment of his approaching crucifixion, perhaps those weeping women in the crowd following him reminded him of Isaiah's words: "Does a woman forget her baby at the breast or fail to cherish the son of her womb? Yet even if these forget, I will never forget you" (Isaiah 49: 14-15). If not, then surely he must have longed to hear that same Voice he heard at his baptism now assuring him, "My precious son, I will never abandon you."

Prayer of the Way of Compassion

O Spirit of solace and compassion,
    as I hurry along my busy way,
    slow me down so I can look twice
    at those with sad, suffering faces.
Cleanse my habit-encrusted eyes
    so I can see Christ in each of them.

Enflame my dulled and cold heart,
    and stir up in me a fierce desire
    to stop and aid my suffering savior.
Plant my feet firmly in a ground of compassion,
    lest at any site of Christ's sufferings
    I blindly stagger by on my busy way.

Infuse your compassion in my heart
    so I may never pass by
    those who are cross-crushed
    without expressing caring and concern,
    without an outstretched hand,
    without even a prayer or blessing
    for my afflicted Lord in need.

+

Let me take up my cross and follow you, Lord Jesus,
for by so doing, I share in the liberation of the world.

THE TWENTY-SIXTH DAY OF THE PILGRIMAGE
Thursday of the Fourth Week in Lent

MEDITATION ON THE CRIMINAL JESUS

We praise you and we follow you, O Christ,
because by our crosses united, we redeem the world.

Scripture for the Twenty-Sixth Day
The inscription of the charge against him read, "The King of the
*Jews." —*Mark 15: 26

Guilty as Charged

At the intersection of El Khanqa Street the Souq Khan al-Zeit
is a mounted plaque stating that at the time of Jesus this site
was the location of the city gate that led out to the countryside.
The plaque also commemorates that at this site the Romans
placed the wooden boards bearing the execution warrants for
condemned criminals. This place, then, is where Pontius Pilate's
execution warrant ordering the crucifixion of Jesus would have
been affixed. A wooden plaque would have been inscribed in
three languages with the crime for which Jesus had been found
guilty; according to Matthew's Gospel it read, "This is Jesus,
the King of the Jews" (Matthew 27: 37). Matthew also says the
warrant plaque was nailed on the cross above Jesus' head, as it
is usually pictured in religious art of the crucifixion. Regardless
of where Pilate's warrant was posted, one thing is certain: It
condemned Jesus to death as a revolutionary, since only Caesar
could be king and ruler of the world.

The road taken by the three cross-carrying criminals led
out of this gate to Golgotha, the Place of the Skull. (In Latin,
the word for skull is *Calvaria*, from which we have the term

Calvary.) It was the destination at the end of death row, the equivalent of the modern-day gas chamber, the end reserved for those who had committed the most dangerous of crimes. Today the three condemned criminals would be called terrorists. They were revolutionaries who had promoted terror by acts of insurrection against the status quo of Rome's occupation of Palestine. The Roman policy was to condemn all rebel-terrorists to death by crucifixion — mere thieves wouldn't have merited this sentence. Contemporary Christians customarily believe that Jesus was innocent of any crime, and yet — at least from the perspective of Roman law — was he truly guiltless? Did not Jesus of Galilee promote complete allegiance to another kingdom that was completely contrary to those existing empires of religion and the imperial state? While he could not be charged as guilty of an armed, violent rebellion, Jesus and his apostle Paul were guilty of initiating perhaps the world's most radical revolution.

Jesus' dramatic prophetic action in Jerusalem referred to as "the cleansing of the temple" was, from another viewpoint, a one-man riot against the temple sacrifice system. With a holy rage he drove the moneychangers and sacrificial animal-sellers out of the temple and so prevented the temple's sacrificial worship, at least for that day. Besides being a serious threat to the Jewish religious structure, his riotous behavior in the temple also constituted an attack on Rome because the temple was under the direct jurisdiction of the Roman occupational authority. Rome's presence in Judea took very seriously this responsibility to maintain law and order in the temple area.

Radically rebellious — whether in Jesus' day or in ours — is the lifestyle that his disciples have been called to embrace. He plainly forbade his followers to engage in any physical acts of violence — even using the weapons of angry words — in response to being attacked. Nor did he provide any escape clause of a just war or holy war justification. Such stringent requirements appear

to sensible people as impossible today as they did in the first century. *(For an expansion of this thought, see the last sections of the* Political Postlogue *beginning on page 236).*

Jesus was, indeed, a religious revolutionary, and his radical teaching included the notion that since God's abode is in the world, and within each person, there should no longer be any need for temples and churches as divine dwelling places. He was clear in saying that even the most sacrosanct religious regulations had to be seen and reinterpreted through the lens of the law of love. Though they did it in a nonviolent way, Jesus and Saint Paul of Tarsus, by laying siege to the absolute power of religion and the state, had to be silenced. So they crucified Jesus and beheaded Paul! In the divine upside-down pattern of paradox, Jesus' execution and the blood that flowed from his wounds nourished the Godseeds he had awakened in his disciples, and instead of his revolution being silenced it was shouted from the rooftops.

Every revolution, even Jesus', is subject to the ravages of aging and, with each generation, loses something of its youthful enthusiasm. The original intoxicating freedom and boldness is diluted until finally the new becomes old and the radical becomes conservative. By centuries of compromises, religion and the state have successfully domesticated the once radically new message of the gospel. Yet, in each age God cries out, "My beloved dream, awaken!" May this Pilgrimage Way of the Cross awaken you to the reality that within you slumbers the Divine Dream. The bloody road of the cross is contagious with a divine disease. It is infected with the mystical malady of divine son- and daughterhood. On this visit to the Holy City do not simply be a religious tourist, become a plaque-struck pilgrim.

On this Death Row Avenue, in the tradition of praying for a happy death, pray instead that at your death site could be posted an official warrant condemning you as a rebel dissident. What would you choose as the charge written on your warrant of condemnation? Consider having your warrant read that you were found guilty of acts of seditious revolution to usher in the kingdom of God, convicted of acts of dissenting from ways of the majority in favor of the ways of God.

Do not be ashamed if you are unable to be as radical as was Jesus of Galilee. Yet surely with God's grace you can be a dissenting disciple, one who, led by the Holy Spirit, is willing to think, speak and act contrary to the majority in order to usher in God's reign.

+

Let me take up my cross and follow you, Lord Jesus,
for by so doing I share in the liberation of the world.

THE TWENTY-SEVENTH DAY OF THE PILGRIMAGE
Friday of the Fourth Week in Lent

THE CHURCH OF THE HOLY SEPULCHER

We praise you and we follow you, O Christ,
because by our crosses united, we redeem the world.

The next four Stations of the Cross are the traditional sites of Jesus' crucifixion, death and burial, all of which occurred out in nature under the great blue dome of the sky. To visit these sacred sites now, however, it is necessary to enter a building, the Church of the Holy Sepulcher. So we go down a narrow street that brings us to the entrance of the church. This large structure gives the impression of being hemmed in by other buildings that are crowded up against it. As a result, the site lacks the majestic sweep of the Jewish Western Wall or the spacious and impressive appearance of the Muslim mosque of the Dome of the Rock.

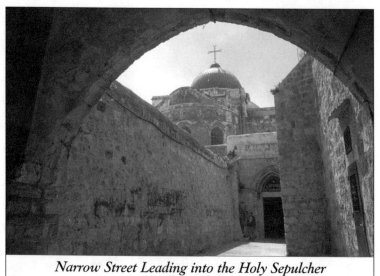

Narrow Street Leading into the Holy Sepulcher

Entering through the one large doorway, we find a dim and ornate environment, crowded with noisy tourists and various groups of pilgrims jostling with one another. All this conspires to rob the most significant church in all of Christendom of its sense of the sacred. Yet from about thirty years after Jesus' death, the Jerusalem community of believers has held the tradition that this was the site of his crucifixion and burial.

The Holy Sepulcher has a long history. These are a few of the highlights: In the first century A.D., the land beneath this stone floor was an unused stone quarry located just outside the walls of Jerusalem. Archaeologists have found tombs underneath this church dating back to the time of Jesus. Sixty some years after the destruction of Jerusalem, in A.D. 135, the Roman Emperor Hadrian built a temple on this site to Venus, the goddess of love. Later, on that same site the Roman Emperor Constantine, at the urging of his saintly Christian mother Helena, built a church to honor the place of the resurrection of Christ. This original church was completed in the year 335, but was destroyed in 1009 by the Muslim Caliph Hakim, the damage completed by an earthquake in 1034. In 1042, it was partially rebuilt with Byzantine funding, and on July 15, 1099, the Crusaders entered the church as the new rulers of Jerusalem. They finished the reconstruction, and today's church is more or less the one refurbished by the Crusaders.

Throughout the centuries Christianity's most sacred church has suffered from fire and the decay of aging, but even more sadly it has been seriously fractured over the ages. The cause of this fracture was not an earthquake or one of the countless political wars in the region. Rather, it was due to the rivalry of various Christian religious rites or churches, each claiming a section of the church as their private property. Right up to the present day their services are often conducted at the same time, in competition with one another, reflecting the contentiousness of their general attitude and behavior. By divine good fortune,

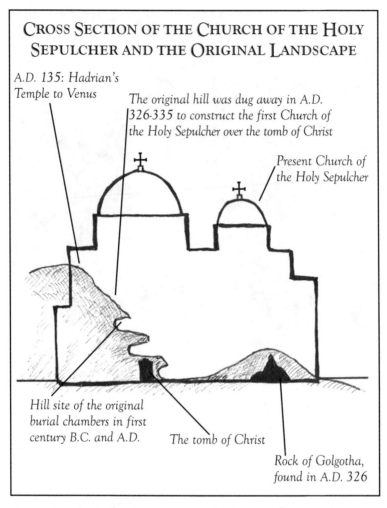

CROSS SECTION OF THE CHURCH OF THE HOLY SEPULCHER AND THE ORIGINAL LANDSCAPE

A.D. 135: Hadrian's Temple to Venus

The original hill was dug away in A.D. 326-335 to construct the first Church of the Holy Sepulcher over the tomb of Christ

Present Church of the Holy Sepulcher

Hill site of the original burial chambers in first century B.C. and A.D.

The tomb of Christ

Rock of Golgotha, found in A.D. 326

the Holy Sepulcher Church is available to all Christians of any sect because of the fact that since the days of the Ottoman Empire (approximately 1400-1600 A.D.) the keys to the door of the Holy Sepulcher have been in the possession of a local Muslim family. What a great paradox that Christianity's holiest site remains open to all Christian denominations because the only entrance is the property of a Muslim and because Israeli police patrol the church area.

Church of the Holy Sepulcher

Inside the Holy Sepulcher Church

Greek Orthodox Catholics occupy the main and largest section of this restored Crusaders' church, where, according to Christian tradition, the center of the world is located. Holding a primary position in this section are the thrones of the Greek Orthodox Patriarchs of Jerusalem and Antioch.

Throughout the other parts of the church are numerous shrines and chapels, including those belonging to the Armenian, Coptic and Latin Rite (Roman) Catholics, with the chapel of the Ethiopian Catholics up on the roof of the Church of the Holy Sepulcher. Reverenced in these various shrine-chapels is perhaps the world's greatest collection of legendary sacred places. Unlike Medieval pilgrims, who were fascinated with relics, today's pilgrim generally only smiles at chapels purporting to be the authentic sites of the cave of Adam, the stone on which the dead body of Jesus was anointed, the tombs of Joseph of Arimathea or the pillar on which Jesus was tied during his scourging. These and other chapels that claim to be the actual sites of significant events in the passion of our Lord can eclipse the church's most important holy place. Located near the center of the church is an unusual marble structure built over the place that has been venerated for 1,700 years as Jesus' burial tomb *(see photo on page 180)*.

Reflection

Other than the Last Supper, all the significant events of the passion and resurrection of Jesus Christ occurred outside in nature. Today, except for the area of his baptism and the garden around Gethsemane, these places of truly holy land must be visited by going inside church structures. The desire to reverence a natural sacred site by enclosing it inside a church has robbed the organic awesomeness of what is called "holy land." God instructed Moses to remove his sandals because the earth where he was standing was holy, made so by God's visitation in the burning bush. Those places of the visitation of Jesus — places where he lived out all the implications of his baptism — are equally holy ground. Visiting these enclosed sites of his passion and resurrection, now often crowded with the sham of gaudy decorations and ungodly divisions, hardly tempts one to remove one's shoes.

Like centuries of pilgrims before you, coming here exposes you to a potential public display of the ugly wounds of division and rivalry among Christians, the sectarian separation that is so apparent in this holy shrine. Adding to that is the absence in this ancient Christian shrine of significant parts of the Body of Christ, for none of the Reformation churches have been allowed their own presence. While able to visit the Holy Sepulcher Church, Protestant pilgrims must worship in their own churches scattered about in the old Holy City.

Jesus, the gospels tell us, wept over the Holy City because it had failed to know the time of God's visitation. The Risen

Christ must still weep over the scandalous competition of Christians over possession of pieces of his tomb site. Souls with ears to hear might make out the Risen One sobbing over his disciples' mutual denunciations and the arrogant claims of superiority in this church.

Might he not say in response, "I'm not buried here anyway, so why wage wars over an abandoned tomb? What is important to me is not building marble shrines to the holy past, but rather living, flesh-and-blood shrines of the holy in the present."

A Pilgrim's Prayer of Exorcism

At your Last Supper, Lord Jesus,
    you passionately prayed for unity,
    pleading, "That you may be one, my friends,
    as the Father and I are one."
Instill in us your passion for unity
    for a communion among your companions.

O Lord, you who once freed
    those possessed by evil spirits,
    come and exorcise our demons
    of crippling religious exclusivity,
    demons of shameful pious superiority
    over those of different beliefs.

Drive out of us any evil spirits
    of prejudice and competition
    against your friends of other churches
    who also love you and your cross.
Thus released, may we rightfully embrace them
    as our beloved brothers and sisters.

Free us, too, of our greedy possession, our sense
    that the cross belongs only to Christians,
    so we may see it as a redemptive gift
    you've given to all peoples,

regardless of their religion,
and even those who lack faith.

Then, we may recognize all those
who daily strive to live justly,
who treat others with compassion
and seek to know the Divine Mystery,
as part of our family
and our true cross companions.

As we now return to our pilgrimage, we move on to where
Jesus was stripped naked before being nailed to his cross.

+

*Let me take up my cross and follow you, Lord Jesus,
for by so doing I share in the liberation of the world.*

The Twenty-Eighth Day of the Pilgrimage
Saturday of the Fourth Week in Lent

Jesus Is Stripped of His Clothing

We praise you and we follow you, O Christ,
because by our crosses united, we redeem the world.

Scripture for the Twenty-Eighth Day

*When the soldiers had crucified Jesus, they took his clothes and divided them into four shares, a share for each soldier. They also took his tunic, but the tunic was seamless, woven in one piece from the top down. So they said to one another, "Let's not tear it, but cast lots for it to see whose it will be." —*John 19: 23-24

All four gospels record how the soldiers stripped Jesus of his clothing; this event is also remembered in the traditional Way of the Cross at the Tenth Station. In our Pilgrimage Way of the Cross it is not a station but a shrine where we will stop and pray.

Strip searches of prisoners or those arrested or held under suspicion of a crime may at certain times be a necessary measure. Unfortunately, this action is often employed as a shaming device, a procedure exercised by guards and police to humiliate those under their control. Living in a very modesty-conscious culture, it surely must have been humiliating for Jesus to have his clothing stripped off and to be forced to stand naked before the mocking crowd. More than embarrassing, such nakedness is demeaning. Those in hospitals and nursing homes who at times are required to remove their clothing know a small measure of the shame Jesus experienced as the soldiers prepared to nail him to the cross.

This shrine reminds us that we imitate those Roman soldiers whenever we strip people of their dignity — perhaps by asking personal questions about their private lives, by pointing out their mistakes or by publicly calling attention to their faults. We certainly repeat the stripping of Jesus whenever we engage in gossip that immodestly strips the good standing of others, as well as by discriminatory humor or slurs. The following prayer is offered for reflection at this shrine.

The Stripping Prayer

Gracious God, Source of all gifts,
   at this sacred shrine, grant me twin graces:
First, may I never strip others of their dignity,
   removing their good name by gossip,
   by groundless accusation or judgment,
   in the process reenacting your Son's naked shame.

Secondly, grant me the grace to accept those times
   when sarcasm or medical necessity
   strips me of my dignity and honor.
Awaken me to my original glorious dignity,
   when I first entered this world nude,
   yet stunningly beautiful in your image.

Whenever some embarrassment
   exposes me uncovered to shame,
   kindle my baptismal memory
   of my body being Spirit-anointed,
   oiled as a royally consecrated person,
   like Jesus, a priest, prophet and king.

So, naked or clothed, beautiful or abused,
   youthful or aged, healthy or ill, living or dead,
   may I be aware that my body always reflects
   the beautiful body of Christ.

+

Let me take up my cross and follow you, Lord Jesus,
for by so doing I share in the liberation of the world.

PILGRIMAGE SUNDAY

The Fifth Sunday in Lent

A Meditation at the Chapel of Calvary

*We praise you and we follow you, O Christ,
because by our crosses united, we redeem the world.*

Having moved apart from the noisy hubbub of the pilgrims and tourists milling about, we pause at the steps leading up to the traditional site of the crucifixion. This chapel is a Shrine to Pain that commemorates the dreadful suffering that culminated in the death of Jesus. In the floor of the Orthodox Cathedral section of the Holy Sepulcher is a marker of the traditionally acknowledged center of the world. Indeed, many ancient maps showed Jerusalem at the center of the then-known world. The Chinese, on the other hand, once believed that the world's center was wherever the emperor was. Regardless of what site you acknowledge as the center of the world — whether in Jerusalem or elsewhere — uncontested is the reality that pain is the epicenter of life.

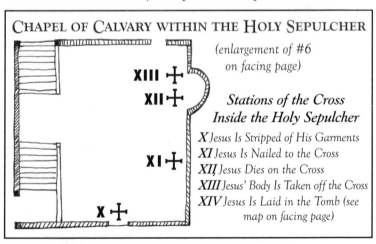

CHAPEL OF CALVARY WITHIN THE HOLY SEPULCHER

XIII ✠

XII ✠

XI ✠

X ✠

*(enlargement of #6
on facing page)*

*Stations of the Cross
Inside the Holy Sepulcher*

X Jesus Is Stripped of His Garments
XI Jesus Is Nailed to the Cross
XII Jesus Dies on the Cross
XIII Jesus' Body Is Taken off the Cross
*XIV Jesus Is Laid in the Tomb (see
map on facing page)*

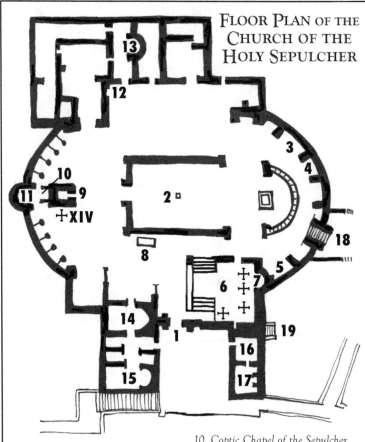

FLOOR PLAN OF THE
CHURCH OF THE
HOLY SEPULCHER

1. Entrance doors
2. Greek Orthodox Cathedral and
   marker of the center of the world
3. Orthodox Chapel of St. Longinus, Roman
   soldier whose lance pierced Jesus' side
4. Armenian Chapel of the Division of
   Clothing
5. Orthodox Chapel of the Mocking and
   Crowning with Thorns
6. Calvary or Golgotha
7. Chapel of Adam, where his skull was
   discovered
8. Stone of the Unction, where Jesus' body
   was anointed
9. Tomb of the Holy Sepulcher
10. Coptic Chapel of the Sepulcher
11. Syrian Chapel of Nicodemus' Tomb
12. Latin Catholic Chapel of
    Mary Magdalene
13. Latin Chapel of the Apparition,
    where Risen Jesus appeared to Mary
14. Forty Martyrs Chapel
15. Greek Orthodox St. John Chapel
16. Coptic Chapel of St. Michael
    and All the Angels
17. Armenian Chapel of St. John
18. Stairs down to the Chapels of
    St. Helena and Finding the Cross
19. Stairs to Ethiopian Coptic Chapel
    and Monastery located on the roof

Life begins with a mother's labor pains and often ends in pain. Between birth and death, pain is ever present. Painkillers are in great demand in our age; it has been estimated that every day Americans alone consume over 76,000,000 Valium pills. Hundreds of millions more attempt to drown the pain of life in alcohol, work and television. Pain is energy, and her twin sister is Pleasure. To those willing to be her students, Pain the professor also teaches invaluable lessons, among them the divine art of compassion. Any personal physical, emotional or soul pain can open you up to share in a holy communion with the suffering of others. In life everyone suffers, yet the vast majority of us forget or mask our pain, and this loss of memory prevents us from sharing others' pain. Compassion is only possible for rememberers.

Such remembering of pain goes against the grain of the mind, whose healing powers erase painful memories so that we can engage in daily life. Yet if we desire deep healing and wish to be truly compassionate, then we need selectively to recall and attend to significant times of pain in our childhood, teenage years, young adulthood and at every stage in life. And here is the heart of our Sunday meditation at the Calvary chapel: The prayerful remembrance of the agonizing death of Jesus fertilizes our personal memories of painful experiences. Each time we pray, "...because by our crosses united, we redeem the world," we are given a holy and healthy reason to remember our wounds.

The Way of the Cross is the Path of Pain. The Way of the Cross teaches that all creative growth requires pain. The sufferings of the Cross mirror the lifelong labor pains required to be reborn by the Spirit. And it's not just at the major traumas of our life. It is also the everyday painful irritation of saying *no* to myself so as to say *yes* to others, the constant, painful suppression of my urge to judge and condemn another.

To embrace your pains, as Jesus did throughout his entire

life and especially here on Calvary, requires the strength and endurance of the meek. Often, the masculine or striving part of us rejects meekness and gentleness as signs of weakness. Yet real inner strength grows out of the ground of gentleness. Only those with strong and brave hearts can endure and transform their agonies — as Jesus did — without whimpering and whining. God the Almighty is also the All-gentle; moreover, God has a preferential option for the meek and powerless. Here on Calvary at the foot of the cross, Mother Mary will hold her dead son's body in her lap. In just such a way, our motherly God cradles the meek, the broken and powerless in the arms of divine compassion and tender love. Becoming Godlike requires the great strength and true compassion that comes from entering into the suffering of the afflicted. Becoming Godlike requires the great strength of being vulnerable.

The German mystic Meister Eckhart said we should remember that all suffering comes to an end and that whatever we might authentically suffer God has already suffered. Our compassionate God is a companion in the pain and suffering of all humanity and all creatures, wild and tame, as well as in the cosmic passion of all creation. The next time pain visits you, remember that it will pass and recall that you never need to bear it alone. Whenever the reality of suffering encompasses you, remember that by his cross Jesus liberated the world from futile pain and suffering. Recalling his charge to us, "Do this in memory of me," join your pain to his passion and convert the negative energy of your suffering into a dynamic source of good for others and for the entire world.

+

Let me take up my cross and follow you, Lord Jesus,
for by so doing I share in the liberation of the world.

Monday of the Fifth Week in Lent

THE TWELFTH STATION
JESUS IS CRUCIFIED

We praise you and we follow you, O Christ,
because by our crosses united, we redeem the world.

Scripture for the Twelfth Station

They brought him to the place of Golgotha, the Place of the Skull. They gave him wine drugged with myrrh, but he did not take it. Then they crucified him and divided his garments, casting lots for them to see what each should have. —Mark 15: 22-24

Jesus did not privatize his pain. He did not hoard it heroically unto himself but gave it as a healing offering for all humanity and all creation. As he died, Jesus' unspoken prayer was, "Your kingdom come, your will be done," and he gave up his life so

God's reign might come more fully. By the labor pains of his cross, he birthed into life his community of love, equality and justice. Nailed to the cross, he embodied his words, "The one who saves his life will lose it; and one who loses his life will save it" (Luke 17: 33), consecrating these words into his flesh and blood. In the supreme act of surrendering, he opened the palms of his hands to be nailed. In this letting go, he released any grip on his life. Whenever you are called to let go of control over your life situation, pray the silent Prayer of the Nailing: Simply open the palms of your hands, exposing yourself to whatever is about to happen and trusting in God's providential care.

The good news of the cross, even in all of its terrible ugliness, is that in our unprotected weakness we can experience the awesome power and glory of God. The gospel of Calvary joyously announces that death makes possible the definitive mystical union between God and us. All love and life require the crucifying act of letting go. The love that exists in friendship and marriage requires letting go of our individual self so as to be fused with another into something new and larger than either person. To become a truly mature adult requires us to let go of childhood and leave the security of family and home. Each succeeding stage of life requires something of the same process.

Forgiveness requires us to let go of any clinging to the injuries caused by another. Conversion, or repentance, that essential requirement for becoming one of Jesus' disciples, involves letting go of a former way of life so as to be gifted with a new one. Being pardoned requires letting go of any notion of achieving forgiveness by one's own efforts. It involves abandoning our sense of unworthiness caused by guilt and shame and then exposing ourselves to God's extravagant love, which has already brought us pardon before we even asked for forgiveness.

True leaders lead by being the first to perform a heroic deed. In this pattern, Jesus never asks us to do anything that he himself has not already done. His dying words on Calvary reveal

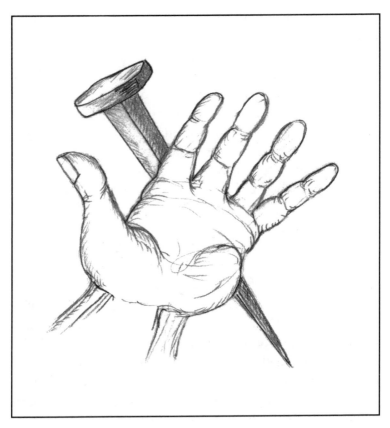

how deeply he was plunged into the doubt-soaked darkness of the absence of God, the Lover he believed would never abandon him. As the end drew near, ominous dark storm clouds gathered over the Hill of the Skull. As hard as he strained to hear, no affirming voice spoke from those clouds at his great Golgotha baptism — only a deadly silence. Right up to the rumble of thunder that concluded Jesus' passion, he remained loyal to his Beloved, neither cursing those who had crucified him nor the God who, it seemed, had abandoned him. The dying, brokenhearted Jesus remained faithful to Love, which then rewarded this fidelity by raising him from the dead. His holy act of opening his palms offers liberation to all of us who fear death.

Prayer of Calvary's Cup

Lord Jesus, you said, "Do not be afraid,"
yet your words seem to say,
"Rise above whatever you fear,"
so as to be liberated from fear's prison.

At Gethsemane you sweated blood,
terrified of Calvary's cup of pain.
Yet you arose to be led away to die,
because you trusted in God's great love.

You arose as they nailed you to the cross
and then ascended from the greatest fear:
abandoning yourself to die alone,
hanging only by a thread to God.

"Come and follow me," you whisper
in a death rattle from your cross.
"Fear not dying alone, for I assure you,
both the Creator God and I will be there."

+

*Let me take up my cross and follow you, Lord Jesus,
for by so doing I share in the liberation of the world.*

THE THIRTEENTH STATION

JESUS PROMISES PARADISE
TO HIS COMPANION CONVICT

We praise you and we follow you, O Christ,
because by our crosses united, we redeem the world.

Scripture for the Thirteenth Station

When they came to the place called the Skull, they crucified him and the criminals there, one on his right, the other on his left.... Now one of the criminals hanging there reviled Jesus, saying, "Are you not the Messiah? Save yourself and us." The other, however, rebuking him, said in reply, "Have you no fear of God, for you are subject to the same condemnation? And indeed, we have been condemned justly, for the sentence we received corresponds to our crimes, but this man has done nothing criminal." Then he said, "Jesus, remember me when you come into your kingdom." Jesus replied to him, "Amen, I say to you, today you will be with me in Paradise." —Luke 23: 33, 39-43

At this station, compassion ascends to heroic strength as the criminal crucified with Jesus gives him solace. The criminal's sympathy required a supreme act of self-denial: rising above one's own agony so as to reach out in kindness to another in great pain. To enter truly into the sufferings of another is difficult enough, but to do it when you yourself are in great agony is amazing. Christian tradition has given the name of Dismas to this convicted revolutionary who was hung on the cross next to Jesus.

It seems clear that the convicted criminal Dismas was a stranger and not one of Jesus' disciples. His expression of acknowledgment and affirmation must have been birthed in that deeper place of the soul where by divine design all humans are family and from which they recognize what is true and good. Yet Jesus and Dismas shared more. They shared the same destiny of dying in a hideous execution and were baptized together in the Great Baptism of Death and Dying. This is the authentic baptism of which Jesus spoke to his disciples, the baptism of which any religious water ritual is only a symbolic mirror. The convict Dismas became the convert disciple by his bloody baptism, which culminated only a few minutes of misery before his death. This condemned convict is an archdisciple, a true heroic follower, who, unlike the apostles and other disciples, intimately participated in Jesus' crucifixion at the very moment it happened.

After consoling Jesus, he did not ask for the gift of salvation but only that he might be remembered once Jesus entered his kingdom. The dying Jesus then telescoped time and space for Dismas, consolidating Good Friday, Easter Sunday and the Final Resurrection Day into a single day. *"This day you will be with me in Paradise."* That promise canonized him as St. Dismas of the Cross, the patron saint of deathbed conversions. He is the evangelist of the truly good news about our death-day, revealing the divine mystery that if we die united with Christ the door of our death opens directly unto Paradise.

As time-bound citizens of this world, each year we celebrate that divine unification of death and resurrection by extending it over the three holy days of Good Friday, Holy Saturday and Easter Sunday. This partitioning of events allows a prayerful absorption of the three stages of dying, being dead, and being raised up as an entirely new creation. In the timeless reality of the divine mystery, however, these three events are compressed into a single blinding moment of ecstasy. When death takes away those whom you love, as an earthbound prisoner of time you suffer their physical absence until you and they are once again united in Paradise. Yet for your deceased beloved, this time of separation passes a thousand times faster than a flash of lightning.

This Thirteenth Station holds a faith-filled farewell gift for those who must say good-bye to dying loved ones. Remembering this station, we can bid them a final farewell, saying, "I promise you, *this day* I will be with you in Paradise."

Prayer of a Compassionate Companion

Love breaks free the icy grip of death.
Love knows not the time-clutch of clocks.
Love spans even beyond cosmic spaces.
Love links together heaven with earth.
Love can honestly say, "This very day,
    I promise you will be with me in Paradise."

St. Dismas, condemned convict,
    compassionate companion of Christ,
    who shared in Jesus' capital punishment
    and joyously participated in his Easter victory
    and his instant ascension into heaven,

from your place in Paradise, intercede for me
that I may be cleansed of my prejudice
against the convict brothers and sisters of Christ.

Lord Jesus, you also promised Paradise to those
who visit you when you are in prison.
Help me to make frequent visits
to you and all the companions of Dismas,
who, for whatever reason, are imprisoned.
May I comfort and companion them
at least by prayer and concern
and with a compassion devoid of judgment.

+

Let me take up my cross and follow you, Lord Jesus,
for by so doing, I share in the liberation of the world.

Visual Reflection

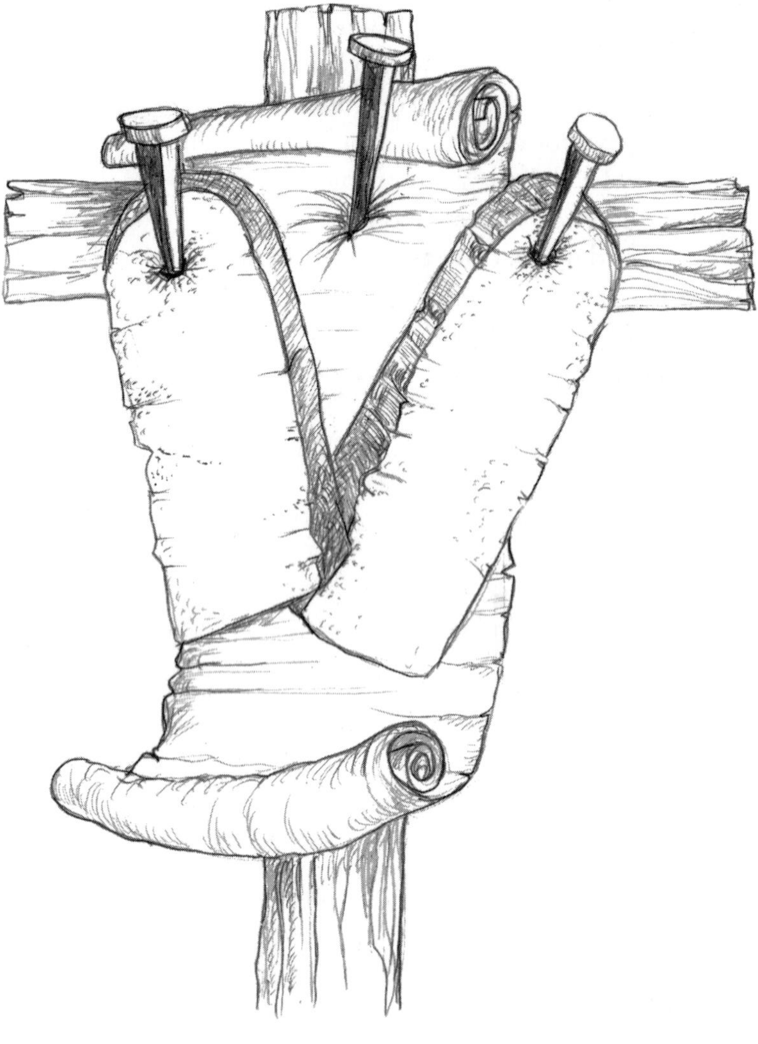

GOD OBLITERATED THE LAW

(God) brought you to life along with him, having forgiven us all our transgressions. Obliterating the bond against us, with its legal claims, which was opposed to us, he also removed it from our midst, nailing it to the cross.

—Colossians 2: 13-14

A Meditation

Saint Paul announced the intoxicating good news that God has blotted out the written ordinances against us, erased the words of our mortgages, freeing us from our sin debts. In ancient times, whenever a law was canceled, it was attached to a board with a nail. So, Paul says that on Calvary God nailed the written law to the cross of Christ, initiating a new age of grace, in which God's law would be written in our hearts.

Remember the crucifixion the next time you are tempted to examine your conscience by reviewing your observance of the ten commandments and all the written laws. Look upon the crucifix and remember that those written laws, along with all your debts, were nailed to the cross with Jesus — and so have been obliterated. Then, examine your conscience for any failings to observe the great law of your heart: love.

Wednesday of the Fifth Week in Lent

The Fourteenth Station

Jesus Speaks to His Mother
and Beloved Disciple

We praise you and we follow you, O Christ,
because by our crosses united, we redeem the world.

Scripture for the Fourteenth Station

Standing by the cross of Jesus were his mother and his mother's sister,
Mary the wife of Clopas, and Mary of Magdala. When Jesus saw his
mother and the disciple whom he loved, he said to his mother, "Woman,
behold your son." Then he said to the disciple, "Behold your mother."
And from that hour the disciple took her into his home."

—John 19: 25-27

At his Last Supper Jesus promised he would not abandon his

disciples as orphans. While his male disciples boasted that they would stay with him to the end, only John and a handful of his women disciples stood the test of the cross. His mother Mary joined with the other two weeping women named Mary and faithfully attended the execution of her criminal son. Steeped as he was in the psalms and the prophet Isaiah, whom he had quoted frequently, one can almost hear the prophet's words as Jesus looked down at his mother standing beneath his cross: "Can a woman forget her nursing child, or show no compassion for the child of her womb? Even though these may forget, yet I will not forget you" (Isaiah 49: 15).

The poignant scene of this Fourteenth Station speaks of the painful process of saying good-bye. Gathered at the foot of the cross, this handful of women followers and the disciple John stood in for all of us who have ever followed the dying prophet of Galilee. To them — and to us — his departing words could again have come from Isaiah: "Do not be afraid, for I have redeemed you; I have called you by name, you are mine.... You are precious in my sight, and honored, and...I love you.... Do not be afraid, for I am with you" (Isaiah 43: 1, 4-5). Seeing their tears and approaching the agonizing end of his life, he could also have repeated the words he spoke at the Last Supper, "Do not let your hearts be troubled or afraid. You heard me tell you, 'I am going away and I will come back to you.' If you loved me, you would rejoice that I am going to the Father" (John 14: 27-28).

In Jesus' actual farewell words to Mary and John he gave them to each other to care for each other. In the mutual love of John and Mary, and in our loving one another, Jesus does return, and is with us. Indeed, in every act of caring and affection, Christ returns — if we are not blinded to these continuous Second Comings by the unbelievable, too-good-to-be-true mystery of the mystical divinity present in all loving.

"Rejoice, for I am going to the Father." If the dying Jesus

had repeated this Last Supper injunction here on Calvary it would have sounded bizarre, for it would have called us to rejoice even in the tragedy of death. Each of us walks the Via Dolorosa whenever we must make funeral arrangements for a loved one, as we stand by the casket at the wake and then walk to the gaping hole of the grave. Only madness or the surfacing of an unconscious and intense dislike for the departed — or remarkable faith — could transform a personal Via Dolorosa into a Via Gaudioso.

Recall that Jesus prefaced his suggestion about our rejoicing in his death by saying, "If you love me." Only by truly loving those who are dear to us, desiring what is best for them, can we, with tearful joy, give them back to the God who only loaned them to us for a short while. This joy is not the same as happiness but, rather, gives delight to our soul because of their new fullness in life. Only by such faith-filled surrendering of those dearly loved can we live out the vow of poverty. This poverty of Calvary, which all disciples are called to embrace, contains the fullness of the blessed joy promised by Jesus, "Happy are those who are poor, for theirs is the kingdom of heaven" (Luke 6: 30).

The dying of Jesus on his cross enfleshed his Last Will and Testament, which he gave to his family of disciples at his last Passover meal: "Do not let your hearts be troubled. Have faith in God; have faith also in me.... If I go and prepare a place for you (in my Father's house), I will come back again and take you myself so that where I am you also may be" (John 14: 1-3). The Risen Christ, the Divine Usher and Easter Escort, promises that he himself will come to our deathbeds to take us home. When you do not simply nod assent to that statement but are convinced that you are a beloved heir to that promised inheritance, then for you every Via Dolorosa becomes a Via Gaudioso.

Prayer of a Final Good-Bye

Infinite Lord of life and death,
    as your son Jesus said good-bye
    to his mother and beloved disciple with great love,
    when that great thief Death breaks into my life,
    when that feared Burglar in Black comes
    to snatch away a dear one,
    one who is my very life,
    may I gather with the weeping women
    at this farewell station
    so that with a whole heart and soul I may stand
    at the sad station of my beloved's bedside cross.

Give me the grace to let my loved one go,
    saying good-bye and not greedily clinging tightly
    out of my own personal and even selfish needs
    or out of my fear at the emptiness of only half a life.
Rather, may I generously give my beloved back to you.

With holy faith, O God, may I disrobe the Thief,
    removing the Burglar in Black's thinly veiled disguise,
    to reveal him as a servant of the Usher of Heaven,
    my Beloved Easter Escort to Paradise.

When Christ the Usher leads my loved one away,
    may my heart, saturated with tear-soaked prayers,
    be filled with a faithful and uncommon joy,
    spun with threads of love and holy loss.

+

Let me take up my cross and follow you, Lord Jesus,
for by so doing I share in the liberation of the world.

Thursday of the Fifth Week in Lent

THE FIFTEENTH STATION
JESUS DIES ON THE CROSS

We praise you and we follow you, O Christ,
because by our crosses united, we redeem the world.

Scripture for the Fifteenth Station

At noon darkness came over the whole land until three in the afternoon. And at three o'clock Jesus cried out in a loud voice, "Eloi, Eloi, lema sabachtani?" which is translated, "My God, my God, why have you forsaken me?" Some of the bystanders who heard it said, "Look, he's calling Elijah." One of them ran, soaked a sponge with wine, put it on a reed and gave it to him to drink, saying, "Wait, let us see if Elijah comes to take him down." Jesus gave up a loud cry and breathed his last. —Mark 15: 33-37

Jesus of Nazareth is the greatest hero of the Christian Western world — and, significantly, one of the few major heroes who was not a warrior or military conqueror. In combating the dark powers and the imperial powers of the state and religion, he engages in the great battle stark naked of any weapons or armor and ultimately loses his life. His crucifixion is the crescendo of courage, the zenith of nonviolent strength that only great love made possible. While his dying, agony-soaked words reveal his feeling that God had completely abandoned him, he did not abandon God. He neither cursed nor rejected the God whom he felt had deserted him. Jesus' orphan death demonstrates history's decisive victory of faithful love, so unconditionally loyal that he endured not only the rejection of those he had ministered to, and the betrayal, denial and abandonment of his closest friends, but even the seeming absence of the Divine Beloved.

Isaiah speaks of God's fidelity: "Like a son comforted by his mother, so will I comfort you" (Isaiah 66: 13). The scandal of the cross is that God did not come to comfort his beloved Jesus when he was most wracked with pain and crushed by shame. Liberation theologian Jon Sobrino says there is an important spiritual lesson for us in Jesus being abandoned by a God who intentionally refused to intercede in his grotesque death. God is addressed in the Creed as Almighty, yet the God of Good Friday is impotent. This powerlessness, Sobrino says, was essential, for Jesus had to be emptied of all comfort and consolation, including the fundamentally grounding reassurance of the Divine Presence, so that he might be completely hollowed out by death.

Besides Jesus' passion and death, hidden in Gethsemane's chalice of suffering was the fear of being entirely forsaken by God. His total poverty of any sense of being loved was the final test of the limits of his love for God. Good Friday is rightfully called "good" because it is the Day of Love. It is fitting that

Friday is named for *Frigg*, the Nordic goddess of love. Moreover, the Roman soldiers who nailed Jesus to his cross would have called that sixth day of the week *die Veneris*, the day dedicated to Venus, the Roman goddess of love and beauty. The dying Jesus, drained of life and the feeling of being loved by God, passionately lives out his incarnation as God's love-in-human-flesh.

God is also enfleshed in you and me, and the death of Jesus provides a model for how we are to love others and God. Such a great love involves a willingness to be emptied out — drained to the last drop. As St. Paul writes, "Have among you the same attitude that was in Christ Jesus, who, though his state was divine, still he did not cling to his equality with God. Rather, he emptied himself and assumed the state of a slave... accepting death, even death on a cross" (Philippians 2: 5-8).

On the cross, Jesus refused the drugged wine offered him because he had already drunk deeply of the wine of God. Mechtild of Magdeburg, the laywoman mystic of the Middle Ages, said that God gives us two wines to drink. One is the white wine of joy and great ecstasy; the other is the red wine of pain and great loss. To live life in great abundance, as Jesus had, requires drinking both of those wines, aware that they blend the twin rich vintages of heaven. Indeed, the feast of life is balanced by the confluence of the white and the red wines of joy and pain.

Throughout his life Jesus had imbibed fully of the joy of God's presence. Now, all along the way of this Bloody Friday, he had to drink his Gethsemane cup filled with sour vinegar that he ardently prayed would pass him by. Nailed on the cross, hanging between heaven and earth, in his final agony he consumed that skull cup to its bitter dregs. Fully drunk with grief, satiated with suffering, he needed no more wine — certainly not wine that would drug his pain. With a piercing soul cry, his life-breath was squeezed from his lungs — and he died.

Prayer of the Emptying Station

Good Friday, Good Monday,
  good whatever day of the week,
  you will be my Final Good Day
  on my own Way of the Cross.
With loved ones, or all alone,
  in a quiet peace, or in torment,
  mentally alert, or unconscious,
  may I die as faithfully as did my Lord.

Death, final station of my life,
  you are no pious filling station,
  you are God's Emptying Station,
  draining me of all that's precious —
  all my joys, loves, home and work —
  so that I can be generously filled up,
  lavishly overflowing, with Life.

May each draining station in my life,
  every heartbreak and sad failure,
  prepare me for my Good Friday,
  when dark death will empty me completely
  so I can be completely filled
  with life, light and love.

+

Let me take up my cross and follow you, Lord Jesus,
for by so doing, I share in the liberation of the world.

VISUAL REFLECTION

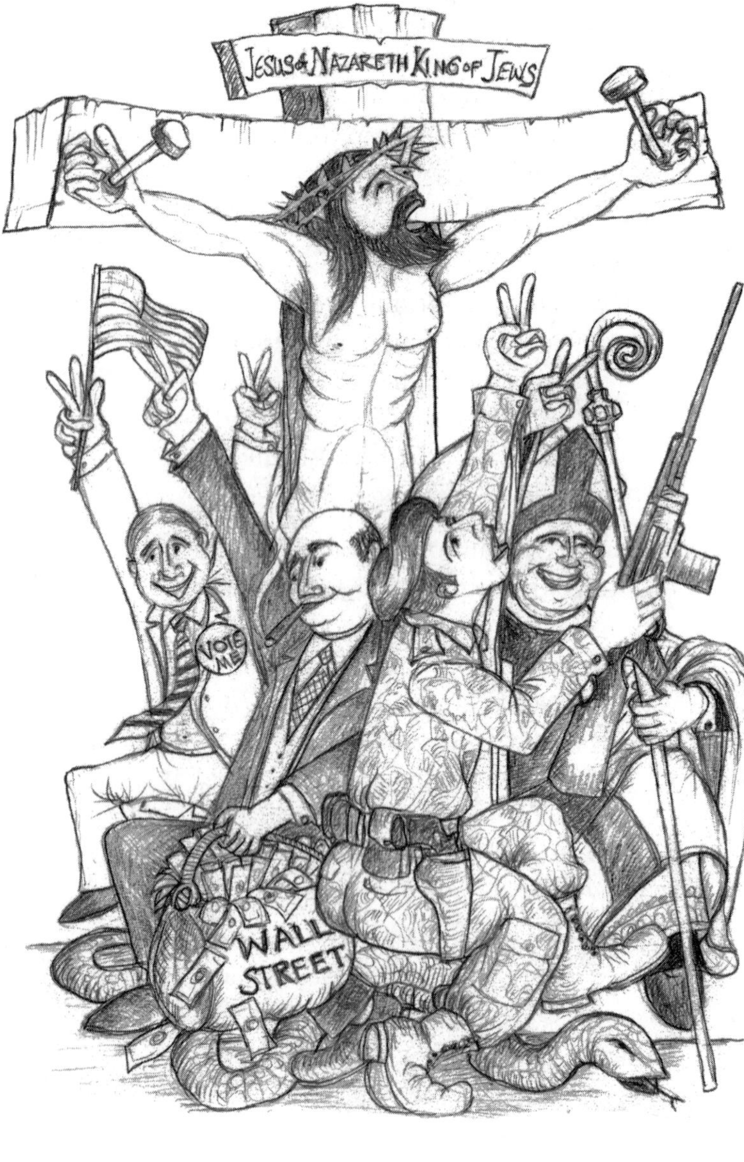

THE FRIDAY VICTORY SNAKE DANCE

The Lutheran pastor Dietrich Bonhoeffer, who died in a Nazi concentration camp, said, "The figure of the Crucified invalidates all thought which takes success for its standard." Indeed, the Crucified Christ seems the most un-American of images, for it proclaims that God prefers defeat to victory and is able to work more good from failure than from success.

The Victory Snake Dance of Calvary celebrates the victory of
> Evil over Good
> War over Peace
> Violence over Nonviolence
> Hate over Love
> Injustice over Justice
> Greed over Charity
> the Powerful over the Weak

Whenever the vulnerable are suppressed and exploited, even in the name of the common good, or a just cause, or the bottom line, or orthodox theological correctness, the Snake Dance Victory of Good Friday is repeated.

Whenever great rejoicing follows military victories in which multitudes of the innocent are slaughtered, or financial victories in which employees and stockholders are left penniless, the Snake Dance Victory of Good Friday is repeated.

Whenever Religion is victorious because heretics are burned at the stake, or those who speak truth about science or theology are silenced "to protect the simple beliefs of the faithful," the Snake Dance Victory of Good Friday is repeated.

Whenever politicians and governments have defeated the opposition by creating anxiety about criminals, or have catered to greed with inappropriate tax cuts, or appeal to flag-waving nationalism instead of justice and peace, the Snake Dance Victory of Good Friday is repeated again.

THE THIRTY-THIRD DAY OF THE PILGRIMAGE
Friday of the Fifth Week in Lent

A MEDITATION ON THE DEATH OF JESUS

*We praise you and we follow you, O Christ,
because by our crosses united, we redeem the world.*

Of the billions of earth's inhabitants who have died, no other single death has so captured the human imagination as the execution of the criminal, Jesus of Galilee. Meditating upon his death can empower you to live prophetically, regardless of the cost. It can inspire you to live a life of humble service, performing acts of hidden heroism, and to face with noble courage a slow and painful death.

The crucifix challenges even those who feel they do not need religion in their lives: the non-churched or the non-synagogued who find and worship God in the temple of nature, by walking in the woods or watching a brilliant sunrise. God is, indeed, dynamically present in these wonders and all other experiences of creation and should be sought there. However, no stunning sunrise — or even ten thousand radiant dawns — could ever empower us to give away our lives for a just cause, to give away our wealth to the poor or, out of love, to die daily in little ways for our families. Regardless of your religion, or lack of one, the crucifix is a potent symbol. The cross with the crucified body of Christ is the ultimate sign of loving fidelity, even unto death, and a sign of the way to live life abundantly.

As death approached Jesus, darkness covered the land. As the sun evaporated into evil ebony, he cried out in agony, surrendering his spirit in death. As he gave up his last breath, the Gospel of Matthew reports, "The veil of the temple was torn in two from top to bottom. The earth quaked, rocks were split, and tombs were opened" (Matthew 27: 51-52).

The temple veil was hung over the entrance of the Holy of Holies, shielding the doorway to the most sacred place of God's Presence. No one other than the high priest — and then only on the Day of Atonement — was permitted to go beyond that 60-foot tall, lavishly rich temple curtain to the sanctuary where God dwelt. At the moment of Jesus' death, however, the curtain was torn in two, and the Presence of God rushed out into the whole world.

Herod's magnificent Temple, with its now-hollow Holy of Holies, would in forty short years be leveled to the ground by the victorious Roman Army. As we have seen, Jesus had been crucified for being a revolutionary, the most radical in all of

Replica of Herod's Temple and the Holy of Holies (tall tower in the center)

history. Among the reasons he was condemned to be executed was his claim that God had no further need of Herod's Temple — or any other sacred set-aside spaces, with their sanctuary priesthoods acting as consecrated custodians of God's pardon and grace.

The reported natural upheavals that accompanied Jesus' death reveal the cosmic nature of his pain. As the mystic Julian of Norwich said, "...when he was in pain we were in pain. All creatures of God's creation that can suffer pain suffered pain with him. The sky and earth failed at the time of Christ's dying because he was part of nature." All creatures suffer pain, even though we humans tend to think our suffering holds greater significance. More than a bare cross, the embodied crucifix is a universal symbol of the divine and human mystery of love and death that infuses all of life. The crucifix, with the dying body of Jesus, is the sign of how God and humanity, together with all of creation, are involved in the redemptive, liberating rebirth of the world. St. Paul spoke of creation's inclusion in God's cosmic birthing: "For all creation awaits...in hope that creation itself would be set free from slavery to corruption and share in the glorious freedom of the children of God. We know that all creation is groaning in labor pains" (Romans 8: 19-22).

This Fifteenth Station of the Cross, which focuses on the death of Jesus, begs to be celebrated out-of-doors in the midst of all creation. As the sun, moon and earth immediately responded to Jesus' crucifixion, all of creation continues to participate in Christ's passion to this very day by its own pain and dying.

May the Holy Spirit of Imagination expand our vision to see Jesus' crucifixion mirrored in the dying away of various species across our planet, in the extermination of clean water, in the devitalizing of our air and in our environment's countless Calvaries. May that new vision regard Easter lilies and rabbits not only as decorative images for Resurrection Sunday but as sacramental symbols of the reality that in God's design all creation shares in the resurrection of Christ.

We are about to depart from the Hill of the Skull and its ugly cross and return to the Via Dolorosa to walk in funeral procession to the tomb of Jesus. As we do, remember that we are Pilgrims of the Via Gaudioso and, thus, should now look upon this ominous pole of shame and pain with eyes of hope and joy. In his dying on the cross, Jesus converted his pain into the fuel for his great journey of departing from his earthly body to be taken upward into the Cosmic Body of God. Writing in his letter to the Ephesians, Saint Paul explained how it was God's plan to sum up all things in heaven and earth in the Risen Jesus: "...raising Christ from the dead and seating him at his right hand in heaven...he put all things beneath his feet and gave him as the head over all things to the church, which is his body, the fullness of the one who fills all things in every way" (Ephesians 1: 20, 22-23). One translation of this passage says that Jesus' risen body has filled the universe in all its parts. Imagine Christ expanding outward throughout the cosmos, saturating all the existing 200 billion galaxies as well as those just being birthed at this moment.

+

Let me take up my cross and follow you, Lord Jesus, for by so doing I share in the liberation of the world.

Pilgrim Departure Note

Leaving the Chapel of Calvary (*see map on page 151*), we will pass the Shrine of the Unction, which contains the slab of stone where tradition says Nicodemus anointed the dead body of Jesus for burial. John is the only gospel writer who has Nicodemus join with Joseph of Arimathea in performing the required Jewish ritual of anointing a dead body. Customarily, at this shrine you can witness the devotion of pilgrims prostrating themselves and kissing the slab of the stone of the anointing. As we pass them, we walk across the Church of the Holy Sepulcher and enter the rotunda. Directly in front of us is a small marble structure that has been revered for over 1,700 years as the tomb of Jesus (*see photo on page 180*).

THE THIRTY-FOURTH DAY OF THE PILGRIMAGE
Saturday of the Fifth Week in Lent

THE SIXTEENTH STATION
THE BURIAL OF JESUS IN THE TOMB

We praise you and we follow you, O Christ,
because by our crosses united, we redeem the world.

Scripture for the Sixteenth Station

When it was evening, there came a rich man from Arimathea named Joseph, who was himself a disciple of Jesus. He went to Pilate and asked for the body of Jesus; then Pilate ordered it to be handed over. Taking the body, Joseph wrapped it in clean linen and laid it in his new tomb that he had hewn in the rock. Then he rolled a huge stone across the entrance to the tomb and departed. —Matthew 27: 57-60

To rediscover the meaning of the cross in our lives also requires that we newly invest in the meaning of the burial and the tomb.

Jesus died covered with dirt, blood, sweat and spittle, yet as Saint Francis of Assisi said, "God is beauty." That which radiates a divine quality from within is beautiful even when it is wrapped in dirt and in decay. By contrast, our custom is to decorate the bodies of our dead with a cosmetic beauty so they will appear alive and merely sleeping. Failing to find any beauty in death, and attempting to honor our deceased, we disguise them with makeup and dress them in their Sunday best. Just as we dispose of wilting flowers, our social bias prevents us from seeing any beauty in aging or dying. Yet God did not dispose of or abandon the dead body of Jesus as he lay in his cave tomb. In the words of the Psalmist:

> If I lie in the grave, you are there.
> If I take the wings of the dawn
> and dwell at the sea's furthest end,
> even there your hand would lead me,
> your right hand would hold me fast.
>
> If I say, "Let the darkness hide me
> and the light around me be night,"
> even darkness is not dark for you,
> and night is as clear as the day.
> —Psalm 139: 7-12

Contrary to our belief, a tomb is ultimately not a place of decay and death; it is an active and fertile agent in the process of birthing something new. Even while the grave may appear to be dark and foreboding, God is present there transforming the tomb into a womb. Hewn out of rock, or dug into the rich soil of the earth, every grave is essential soil for the seed of life to sprout and grow. As Jesus said, "Unless the grain of wheat falls to the ground and dies, it remains just a grain of wheat; but if it dies it produces much fruit" (John 12: 24). Just as the dark soil of the earth is dynamically alive, providing the rich environment that enables seeds to grow, so also the dark soil

Chapel of the Tomb of Christ in the Holy Sepulcher

of fear can be fruitful for the growth of courage. The black pit of despair can give birth to a fresh and resilient hope, and the soil of the tomb's dust and ashes can produce a harvest of life a hundredfold. The early apostolic bishop St. Irenaeus said, "God became a human being in order that human beings might become God." For that Godseed to sprout and flower fully, death and burial, or cremation, is required. Meister Eckhart said that within each of us is a Godseed. Nature reveals that pear tree seeds when buried in the soil sprout and grow up into pear trees, and apple seeds grow into apple trees. So, too, Eckhart says, the seed of God within grows into God. As the life of Jesus shows, this sacred process begins to take root and flourish long before burial. When the soil of our life is richly fertilized by love and turned over frequently by acts of dying to self, it becomes the flower bed in which our Godseed sprouts and flowers.

On Good Friday afternoon as the sun was beginning to set, the first faithful disciples of Jesus departed from his tomb and surely must have wept, as we do when we bury our beloved dead. Our tears, however, are not a sign of any lack of faith, not a breakdown of belief in the promise of sharing in the resurrection of Christ. Rather, like the tears of Jesus at the tomb of his good friend Lazarus of Bethany, our tears at the grave are sacramental indicators of the depth of our love. Such tears of love water the seeds of life in the final stage of our loved ones' process of bearing fruit. At this Sixteenth Station, marked in the Church of the Holy Sepulcher by the Chapel of Christ's Tomb, we pray as well for the infinite fruitfulness of our own death.

+

Let me take up my cross and follow you, Lord Jesus,
for by so doing, I share in the liberation of the world.

THE SIXTH SUNDAY OF THE PILGRIMAGE

Palm Sunday

A REFLECTION ON THE VIA DOLOROSA:
A DEAD-END WAY

We praise you and we follow you, O Christ,
because by our crosses united, we redeem the world.

The Via Dolorosa and the traditional Stations of the Cross ends
here at the sealed tomb of Jesus. Indeed, the fact that the medieval
Way of the Cross ended at this site of the entombment of Jesus'
dead body explains why it was called the Way of Sorrows. The
Fourteenth and final Station in the old Way of the Cross, then,
can easily be a shrine to despair and defeat that casts a dark shadow
over every tomb. Since it is the last place that we have contact
with our dead, a gravesite can assume a disproportionate
importance that overshadows our faith. What happens at death
is, and will ever remain, an awesome mystery. As a result of our
incomplete understanding of death and our lack of a clear
scriptural definition about it, two different beliefs are proposed
about the resurrection. One school of theologians maintains the
long-acknowledged belief that the dead do not experience their
share in Christ's resurrection until the end of the world and the
Second Coming of Christ. This belief makes cemeteries into
resting places where the dead sleep in peace until their
resurrection. On the other hand, there are theologians, such as
Karl Rahner, who maintain that the resurrection occurs at the
moment of an individual's death. This is particularly appealing in
our day when science acknowledges that time does not exist in
infinity. As it was for Jesus and St. Dismas, resurrection and
complete union with the Divine occur at the moment of death.

This understanding of the resurrection shapes a different attitude toward cemeteries and gravesites. While we lovingly care for and show reverence for these places of burial, we know they do not contain our holy dead resting in peace, for the dead are now assumed into the fullness of God's life and live with God.

We honor the graves of saints, martyrs and those who freely gave their lives for some noble cause, and these sites are visited as religious shrines. We have national shrines at the tombs of known and unknown soldiers and military heroes. These are ceremonially guarded as the precious shrines of those who have fallen in battle and have given their lives for their country. Likewise, all of us on this Pilgrimage Way of the Cross are well aware that over the centuries Christianity has shown great reverence for the tomb of the greatest hero savior, Jesus of Nazareth. This tomb has been guarded by priests keeping watch among countless flickering lamps, as long lines of pilgrims come to touch, kneel at, pray at and kiss his tomb. The difference between the Tomb of the Unknown Soldier and the Tomb of the Known Savior in the Holy Sepulcher, however, is that the latter is empty of both soul and body! That difference, rooted in a gospel understanding, remarkably appears to have been missed by the popes who launched the Crusades to capture Jerusalem and by all the Christian armies who have waged bloody wars to regain possession of Jesus' empty tomb. It has continued to be overlooked through the centuries by the sectarian churches that have engaged in sometimes fierce and bitter conflicts over which one would be the custodian of an empty hole in the rock.

The location of the tomb of the great prophet Moses is unknown. The shrine of Moses is reverenced by devout Jews in their hearts. Like Jesus, Moses and all the prophets live on in what they said and did. For pilgrims of the Spirit, the actual tomb sites of these heroes are unimportant, for their words, deeds and spirit are their living shrines. To visit the best shrine to Jesus of Galilee, you need not travel as a pilgrim to Jerusalem, you only have to open up your New Testament and begin to read the gospels. In the prayerful shrine of your home, pour over his words, reflect on his deeds and then strive to practice what you read. Jesus never requested that we make pilgrimages to his tomb; he did, however, plead that we live out his radical teachings. Become a gospel pilgrim, who daily strives to enflesh Jesus' teachings as fully and with as much love as possible. This will make you an authentic pilgrim of the cross.

PALM SUNDAY EVENING

The Procession of Palms and giving blessed palms make up the ritual of this last Sunday in Lent. In contemporary society this procession is normally reduced to walking-in-place, simply standing and holding a palm branch in your hand during the reading of the Passion. Yet you can easily expand this meaningful ritual, for every day of your life should be a Palm Procession as you process off to work, school, the office or any engagement. Like Jesus' joyful disciples who waved palm branches, laid their clothing across the road and shouted their belief and praise, you can follow the prophet from Galilee to his death in Jerusalem. He rode down from the Mount of Olives into the Holy City as a nonviolent revolutionary, a vulnerable and meek Messiah. Each day offers you the possibility of participating in that palm procession when, as a loyal disciple, you walk in his living way of nonviolent, peaceful conflict with the forces of evil. Today's disciples should cry out their affirmation of Jesus by bold deeds that speak louder than shouts of praise.

+

Let me take up my cross and follow you, Lord Jesus,
for by so doing, I share in the liberation of the world.

Monday of Holy Week

The Seventeenth Station

Jesus Is Raised from the Dead

We praise you and we follow you, O Christ,
because by our crosses united, we redeem the world.

Scripture for the Seventeenth Station

When the Sabbath was over, Mary Magdalene, Mary, the mother of James, and Salome brought spices so they might anoint him. Very early when the sun had risen, they came to the tomb. They said to one another, "Who will roll back the stone for us from the entrance to the tomb?" When they looked up, they saw the stone had been rolled back; it was very large. On entering the tomb they saw a young man in a white robe sitting on the right and were utterly amazed. He said to them, "Do not be amazed! You seek Jesus of Nazareth, the crucified one. He has been raised; he is not here. Behold the place where they laid him." —Mark 16: 1-6

"He has been raised." Those four powerful words have reverberated like rolling thunder down through twenty centuries, continuously challenging the iron-clawed grip of death. On that Sunday morning he was raised up by the Spirit of God, Life Eternal, Life Ever Youthful, out of the utter darkness of death's dormitory in that tomb outside of Jerusalem. We enter this Holy Week by reflecting on the resurrection so we can see all the events of this week from the perspective of that greatest event in human history. What began in a divine instant on the first Good Friday, we now slow down to a day's pace so we might ponder the mystical implications of the Paschal Mystery. As his mother held her dead son in her lap, God also cradled Jesus' lifeless body, aching to recreate Eden's first blinding spectacular sunrise. Imagine God leaning over and passionately kissing his beloved dead Son. At that instant, the sun sprang dazzlingly out of the darkness, and Jesus of Nazareth became the *Christ* – in Greek, "anointed one." Throughout this pilgrimage we have generally referred to the prophet carpenter of Nazareth simply as *Jesus*, since he only became the *Christ* when he was raised up from the dead.

The Anointed Risen Christ is the Morning Messiah, the gift of God announcing a new day, a new humanity and a new creation. The Christ did not simply step out of his tomb, as is pictured in most religious art. Rather, like the rising sun, the Anointed One exploded outward with ecstatic joy in every direction into all the universe, saturating everything that is and that will be. Since that original Easter sunrise, the Divine Reality has kissed with lavish love all creatures and all creation. Along with old Zechariah, we can greet each new day with a passionate prayer: "the daybreak from on high will visit us to shine on those who sit in darkness and death's shadow, to guide our feet along the path of peace" (Luke 1: 78-79). It is difficult for some to believe in the resurrection, but such a belief is second nature for those who profess the Creed of Love. Easter requires no leap of faith for those who have known what it is to be loved, for Easter is the preeminent feast of love. If you possessed the power to restore a loved one to life, would you do it? Even more, if you had the power to enhance a loved one's beauty and life beyond all imagination, would you do it? The Resurrection celebrates a divine love so passionate, infinitely loyal and immensely powerful that God would never allow a beloved to remain in the tomb.

Easter, then, is the Fountain of Life, holding the secret of how to live always with abundant life. It calls us to be joyful disciples of the Via Gaudioso, for as Paul reminds us, if we have shared in the passion and sufferings of Christ, so we shall also share in his resurrection and glory (see Romans 6: 8). Throughout this pilgrimage we have taken up our crosses and followed the thorn-crowned, bleeding Jesus. So we can now marvel that the Divine Lover will one day gloriously raise us up to new life just as Christ was raised. Easter should, therefore, urge us to undress – like the Risen Jesus, who left his burial clothes behind in the tomb. This Seventeenth Station echoes the Eleventh Station, when Jesus was stripped of his garments. As Paul said to the newly baptized, "You have stripped off your old behavior (lifeless burial clothes) with your old self, and you have put on a new self...renewed in the image of its creator. Here in that image there is no room for distinctions between Greek and Jew, between the circumcised and uncircumcised, or between barbarian, Scythian, slave and free man. There is only Christ: He is everything and he is in everything" (Colossians 3: 9-11).

Easter disciples are believers who are "still wet behind the ears." That expression is used for someone as innocent in the ways of the world as a newborn baby. Disciples "still wet behind the ears" are not inexperienced or naive, but just as the last place to dry on a newborn calf or colt is the small indentation behind each ear, these disciples are still damp from their baptismal bath. Years after their baptism, even if it happened as an infant, they remain as dedicated and enthusiastic as when they were towel dried by their godparents. Such freshly alive, deeply damp disciples remain ready to disrobe themselves of any behaviors that make distinctions between male and female, rich and poor, saints and sinners or Christians and non-Christians. Because of their baptismal incorporation into the Resurrection, they have become each of these and more — in Christ. They are eager to discard any attitude-article of attire that might prevent them from being naked of cultural, social and religious biases. To live as still-damp Easter disciples who are alive to the great cosmic reality of their baptism — even while residing among the walking dead — may be the greatest challenge of faith and love.

Prayer of Easter Life

O God of Life, we boldly trumpet our praise
    to you, our God, who fulfills all your promises,
    for what you pledge you always bring about,
    as the glorious resurrection of Jesus proves.
His liberation from the tomb fills us with great hope,
    for we, his disciples, have been promised the same.

Alleluia is our shout to the heavens,
    for the body of Jesus in the tomb
    was just that of a single crucified Jewish man.
Yet your Spirit raised up in Easter glory
    an eternally alive Body of Christ,
    a new creation, male and female,
    of every nation, tribe and religion,
    cosmically one with all of creation.

Our hearts explode with joyous gratitude
    that we share life in the Body of Christ,
    that by baptism we *are* the Body of Christ.
We rejoice in the life the Risen One guarantees,
    freedom from death, life endlessly into infinity.
Alleluia, Alleluia, give us the grace to live fully, each day,
    this glorious Easter life.

+

Let me take up my cross and follow you, Risen Lord Jesus,
for by so doing, I share in the liberation of the world.

Visual Reflection

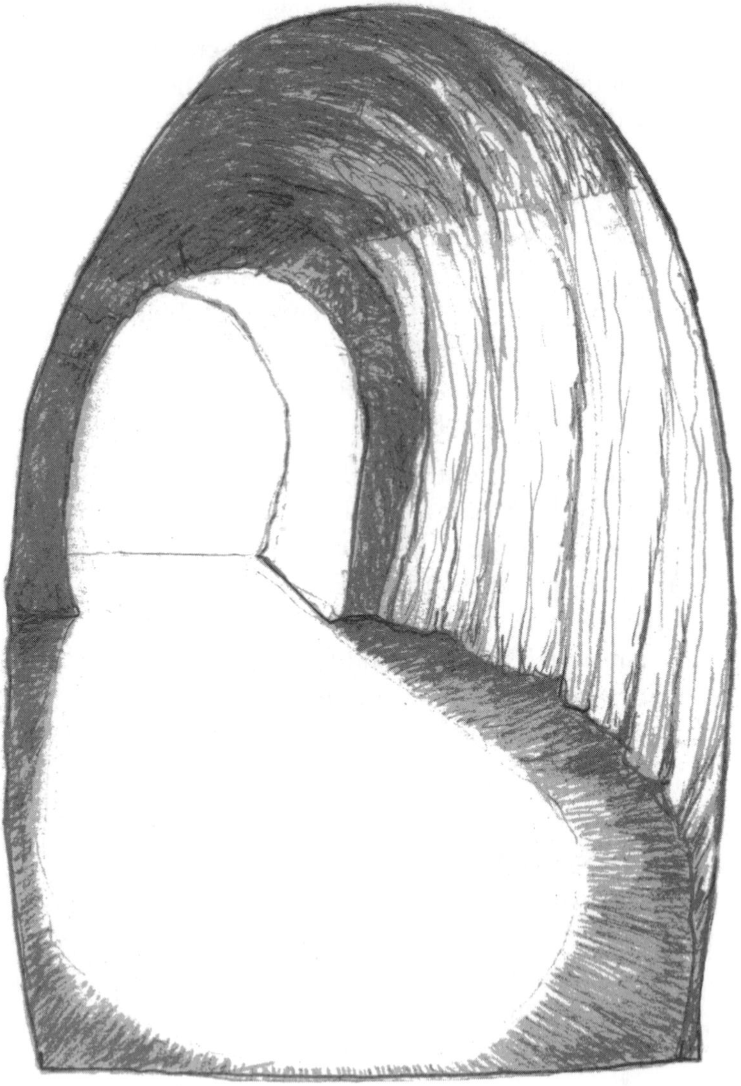

EASTER PROMISE SUNDAY

Finding the tomb of the dead Jesus to be empty was a double discovery. The first was that his body had been stolen, just as the women had feared, but that the thief was his beloved God! The second discovery was that the empty tomb was actually full, saturated with the Promise Fulfiller. God had promised Jesus that if he would be faithful in life — and in death — he would be raised up from the dead. The empty tomb of Jesus became the new Holy of Holies, where the presence of God — one of whose names is Promise Fulfiller — dwells invisibly.

The Holy of Holies of Solomon's Temple contained the Exodus Ark of the Covenant that the Babylonians stole when they conquered Jerusalem and destroyed the Temple. King Herod rebuilt the temple, complete with a magnificent Holy of Holies; yet this new sacred space was completely empty — except for the presence of the Divine Mystery. The abandoned tomb of Jesus in the hillside near Calvary was similarly empty — except that it was filled with the promise of the Divine Presence. In the same way, the grave or tomb of every faithful disciple of Jesus is also empty and yet filled with the Promise Fulfiller. For that promise says that if we share in Christ's death, we shall also share in his resurrection.

THE THIRTY-SIXTH DAY OF THE PILGRIMAGE
Tuesday of Holy Week

A REFLECTION ON LEAVING THE TOMB

We praise you and we follow you, O Christ,
because by our crosses united, we redeem the world.

This Seventeenth Station of the Cross is the last one located inside the Church of the Holy Sepulcher. Before we depart, recall what once existed at this site. Since A.D. 45, only twelve years after his resurrection, the tradition of the devout followers of the Risen Jesus has accepted this as the location of his tomb, which the first disciples found empty on the third day. By the year A.D. 66, most of his Jerusalem disciples had fled for their lives to Pella, located east of the Jordan River. After the Roman Army destroyed Jerusalem in A.D. 70, the Emperor Hadrian rebuilt a new city over the site, a Roman city that he named Aelia Capitolina. It was larger than the original Jerusalem, its new city walls expanding beyond the hill of Calvary. It was also at this time that Hadrian constructed a temple dedicated to Venus on the spot of Jesus' crucifixion and burial.

How appropriate that Hadrian would select this place for a temple honoring the goddess of erotic beauty and sensual love! When we're told that God loves us, we naturally presume that this is a spiritual love, God being spirit. Yet God loves us as passionately as any human lover, cherishing us with great lust! Over time, the once-beautiful words *lust* and *erotic* have become tainted because of how they have been used by sexual exploiters, and because of our prevailing religious discrimination against sexuality. Today lust carries the meaning of excessive sexual craving, while originally it meant "with great pleasure and delight." The adjective erotic, referring to sexual love, comes from Eros, the name of the Greek god of love, better known to us as Cupid, the Roman god of sensual passion. Indeed, the Resurrection celebrates the power of love, including the sensual, bodily dimension. God did not simply raise up the immortal soul of Jesus, leaving his physical body in the tomb to rot. Easter is divinely erotic, for it celebrates how God so delights in creation as to desire to resurrect all of it into a new and imperishable form. Each time we pray the Creed, we profess this divine delight: "We believe in the resurrection of the body." This Godly pleasure in all that is physical has its origin in the moment of Eden ecstasy when God looked upon all that had been created, including the beautiful human bodies of the first man and woman, and "found it very good."

This original pleasure of God, once again manifest in the Easter victory of the bodily resurrection of Christ, has been suppressed over the succeeding centuries by a theology of original sin that has sought to make shameful what God continues to find sensually beautiful. Truly celebrating Easter requires our recovering the beauty we cover up out of shame. Christ's glorious resurrection frees us to view our bodies and sexuality in the same way that God looks upon them. To assist in our liberation from old, negative and impure ways of viewing our bodies, let us return to the image of the Roman goddess Venus. Legend says that Venus was born out of the foam of the sea. In Botticelli's famous painting, a naked Venus is depicted standing on a large seashell as she rises up out of the sea, surrounded by human figures symbolizing the winds lifting her toward the shore. While her sea-birth is a symbolic, mythic birth, it also is a beautiful image of Christian baptism, during which the waters of rebirth are sometimes poured upon us from a silver seashell. From the perspective of our understanding of Baptism, Botticelli's uplifting wind becomes the Holy Spirit, in whom we are plunged into the death and rising of Christ and then swept back onto the shore of daily life. To believe in Easter is to believe in the ongoing transformational powers of our baptism, by which we become a new person. In the early church, candidates entered the baptismal pool naked, symbolic of stripping themselves of their former selves and ways of life. Each Easter celebration requires becoming a new person by stripping ourselves of the centuries of old, disapproving, shame-stained and sin-laden theologies that condemn human sensuality and sexuality.

One more comment before we depart from Calvary. About the year A.D. 326, the Roman Emperor Constantine began his construction of the first church on this site. While not yet baptized, an act that he delayed until he was on his deathbed, Constantine was influenced by his devout Christian mother Helena to establish the new Christian religion as the official religion of the Roman Empire. Within this church of the Holy Sepulcher there is still a Chapel of St. Helena located on the lowest level, accessible by descending a long flight of stairs *(see page 151)*. At the bottom of these stairs is the place — inside a cave near the crucifixion site — where tradition says she found the "True Cross" in 326. It is appropriate that her chapel lies at the foundation of the Church of the Holy Sepulcher, for her lifelong prayer for the conversion of her emperor son is as strong an image of the transformational power of Baptism as Botticelli's Venus.

+

Let me take up my cross and follow you, Risen Lord Jesus,
for by so doing I share in the liberation of the world.

Pilgrimage Directions upon Leaving the Holy Sepulcher

While the new Biblical Stations of the Cross conclude with a Fifteenth Station dedicated to the Resurrection, our Pilgrimage Way of the Cross continues even beyond this point. Departing from the Church of the Holy Sepulcher, our way

Crowd Outside the Church of the Holy Sepulcher

changes to a Pilgrimage Way of the Triumphant Cross. Retracing our path down the narrow, alley-like Souq Khan al-Zeit (see map on page 118), we now walk it with alleluia joy as the Via Gaudioso, for "Christ is Risen!" Plunging back into this crowded street, we find it a surging sea of faces from all lands and places: Arab, Jew, Greek, European, African, Asian, and those from all the Americas. With new eyes of faith, we now see in each face the image of Christ. The noisy hustle and hawking of the business in the marketplace has now ceased to be a distraction from God and prayer. By the death and rising of Christ, this bustle of human business has been transfigured into a holy dwelling place of the Divine, as much as the Holy of Holies of the great Temple. Easter eyes no longer see the ancient division lines between sacred and secular; from now on we can never again perceive anything simply as secular. All is transformed in such seeing.

Upon reaching David's Street, we turn right and walk westward toward the Jaffa Gate. At the Citadel, we turn left down the Armenian Patriarchate Street toward Mt. Zion (see map on page 55). Passing the Cathedral of St. James and going through the Zion Gate, we come to the house of the High Priest Caiaphas. Then, turning left, we arrive again at the Cenacle of the Last Supper. We will visit this shrine a second time, only now as the Eighteenth Station in our new Pilgrimage Way of the Triumphant Cross. Ascending the worn stone steps to the second floor of the building, we again enter the Upper Room.

Wednesday of Holy Week

THE EIGHTEENTH STATION

THE RISEN JESUS CHRIST VISITS HIS DISCIPLES

We praise you and we follow you, O Christ,
because by our crosses united, we redeem the world.

Scripture for the Eighteenth Station

On the evening of that first day of the week, when the doors were locked where the disciples were, out of fear...Jesus came and stood in their midst and said to them, "Peace be with you." When he had said this, he showed them his hands and his side. The disciples rejoiced when they saw the Lord. Jesus said to them again, "Peace be with you. As the Father has sent me, so I send you." When he had said this, he breathed on them and said to them, "Receive the Holy Spirit. Whose sins you forgive are forgiven, and whose sins you retain are retained."
—John 20: 19-23

Because this is a most significant station in the Pilgrimage Way of the Triumphant Cross, it will have an added reflection. The preface to this station begins at sunrise on that cosmically critical first day of the week when Mary of Magdala was weeping at the empty tomb in the garden. Looking up, she saw a man nearby whom she thought was the gardener, and she asked him where he had taken the body of Jesus. When he called her by name, she recognized this stranger to be her beloved Lord. She was so thrilled by the sight of him that she apparently embraced him, for the Risen Christ said, "Do not hold on to me, for I have not yet ascended to the Father. But go to my brothers and tell them, 'I am going to my Father and your Father, to my God and your God'" (John 20: 17).

Recall how on Good Friday Jesus promised Dismas, "*This day* you will be with me in Paradise," joining the events of the Crucifixion and the Resurrection. This day likewise telescopes all the post-resurrection occurrences recorded in the gospels. Within the actual Easter Event, then, are contained each of the appearances of the Risen Jesus to his disciples, as well as the Resurrection, Ascension and the gift of the Spirit.

As we turn to the scene of this Eighteenth Station, we witness the first time Jesus appears to the twelve following his resurrection. Having left Mary of Magdala and ascended to God, the Risen Christ is glorified and so now is able to return on Easter evening to bestow the Pascal Pentecostal gift of the Holy Spirit upon his disciples. They are prisoners of fear, shame and guilt, hiding behind tightly locked doors in their hideout in this upper room. The Risen One releases and liberates them by breathing upon them the gift of the Holy Spirit, for as St. Paul tells us, "Where the Spirit of the Lord is, there is freedom" (2 Corinthians 3: 17).

His greeting, "Peace be with you," is more than a social salutation, it is an absolution for the disciples' sin of desertion, a gentle pardon of their failure to love boldly. The source of his serene pardon is the unconditional, passionate love for them that he had expressed in this very room on the night before his death. Rather than a natural desire for revenge or the need to reprimand them, it is this human love for them, now divinely transfigured, that draws the Risen Jesus like a magnet to their upstairs hideout.

Three nights before, in this very upper room, he had poured out this love to them in his body and blood at the Last Supper. Now he pours out his Spirit upon them. In this Pascal Pentecost, Easter and Eden are fused together. As God had breathed the breath of life into Adam, so the Christ now breathes new life into his fearful, paralyzed followers. The Risen One raises up his friends buried in the graves of their guilty remembrance; as he does so, he makes flesh the words of Isaiah, "Do not remember the events of the past; consider not the things of old. See, I am doing something new" (Isaiah 43: 18-19).

The Galilean carpenter prophet has become the Easter prophet, who is the Inspirer, the Breath-Giver of the Spirit. Walter Brueggeman says that prophets have two functions: One is criticizing and the other is energizing. While alive, the prophet Jesus often criticized the failures of institutional religion and those hypocritically religious people who were sanctimoniously blind to the sufferings of the poor and outcast. He prophetically criticized scriptures that gave permission for the taking of an eye for an eye in revenge, replacing them with a law of love. He criticized antiquated social and religious boundaries by freely violating them when love required it.

Through his resurrection the Risen Jesus now becomes an energizing prophet of the Spirit of Newness. He completely bypasses the previous priestly temple ritual required for the forgiveness of sins and initiates a new person-to-person sacrament, "Whose sins you forgive are forgiven." By this announcement of a new forgiveness, Christ does more than delegate divine power to his disciples — he baptizes them! Both the acts of being forgiven and of pardoning others are experiences of being plunged into the reality of Jesus Christ, who is the forgiveness of sin once and for all. Though we sin again and again, personally repeating the behavior of those first disciples who turned away from Jesus and fled, the forgiveness of Christ is always available. We imitate their cowardly choice to save themselves each time we betray a loved one or reject God by choosing something of this world that takes us away from the way of love. Each turning away requires a return — just as the Risen Jesus returned to pardon his friends with peace. Each act of repentance and forgiveness freshly renews the meaning of the absolution of the Upper Room, which, as we saw, is really the return of Love. Each time forgiveness is extended by a priest or minister, or by a friend to a friend or a spouse to a spouse, the sacred gift of Love returns. It is not delegated juridical power but the power of Love that grants this new forgiveness of the kingdom. It flows from the radioactive reservoir of baptismal grace that resides in the community of Christ's disciples.

Jordan John the Baptizer said that when the Messiah came he would baptize not with water but with the Spirit and fire. The Easter fire that appears in the Upper Room on the evening of the resurrection is the furnace-like presence of the Risen One. Into this furnace of love those first disciples are baptized in the Spirit. Ever since that Easter evening baptismal rite, each anointing in baptism is an ordination of a priestly person as an energizing prophet who has the power to recreate the world with ever-fresh love and creativity. Just three nights before in this same Upper Room, Jesus of Nazareth had created a new covenant by pouring out his blood for all humanity, and now as the Risen Anointed One he initiates the pouring out of the Spirit also upon all humanity. This Easter gift of the Spirit, continued on Pentecost and given in each Baptism, is intended to extend beyond Christians. We of this age are only beginning to perceive the cosmic implications of the Pentecost process begun in that Upper Room. Through it, God has generously poured the Spirit upon Jew, Moslem, Hindu, Buddhist and upon all humanity. Renewing the face and life of the earth is the ongoing work of the Spirit, with whom all anointed Spirit-generators are co-workers. This global outpouring is increasingly essential, because transforming the earth into a world of the justice, peace and love of God is too titanic a task to be accomplished only by those of a single creed or religion!

+

Let me take up my cross and follow you, Lord Jesus,
for by so doing I share in the liberation of the world.

Visual Reflection

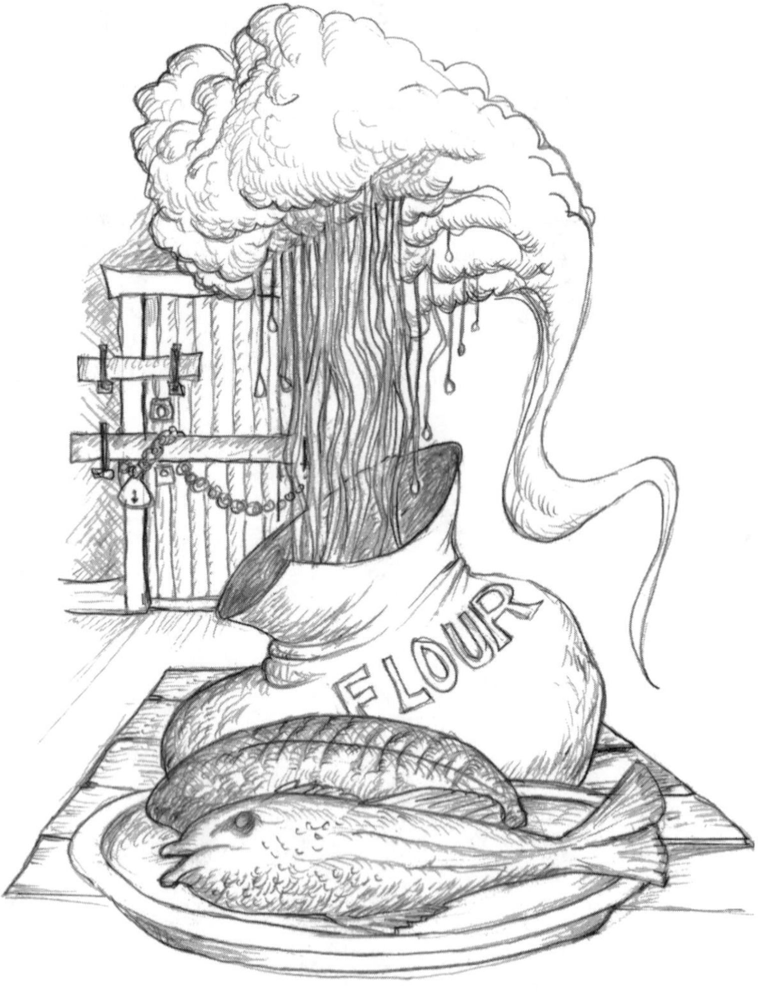

THE PASCHAL PENTECOST
OF THE UPPER ROOM

St. Irenaeus, a second century bishop, envisioned the Holy Spirit as *water*, that essential ingredient in the making of bread. "Like dry flour, which cannot become one lump of dough, one loaf of bread, without moisture, so we who are many could not become one in Christ Jesus without the water that comes down from heaven." On Easter night the Risen Christ poured forth a spring shower of the Spirit upon that fearful lump of dry flour that was his band of disciples, and he transformed them into the bread of life. As fish — which the Risen One also shared with them that night — cannot live out of water, so without the water of the Spirit we cannot become the daily living bread of the kingdom. Thus, on Easter night the Risen One inaugurated the *rain* of God.

THE THIRTY-EIGHTH DAY OF THE PILGRIMAGE
Holy Thursday

SHRINE OF THE LAST SUPPER

We praise you and we follow you, O Christ,
because by our crosses united, we redeem the world.

Scripture of the First Supper

He stood in their midst and said, "Peace be with you." But they were startled and terrified.... And he showed them his hands and his feet. While they were still incredulous for joy and were amazed, he asked, "Have you anything here to eat?" They gave him a piece of baked fish; he took it and ate." —Luke 24: 36-37, 40-43

Before his death Jesus had said, "The last shall be first." Those words became a reality in this room of the Last Supper that is now the room of the First Supper of the Risen Jesus, a Eucharist

Early Church Mosaic of Bread and Fish

of fish and bread. Apostolic tradition holds that both these meals were eaten in this room. This Upper Room table on which was shared the love feast of the soon-to-die Jesus is also the table of the new love feast of the Risen Jesus. The First and Last Suppers are, therefore, forever intertwined, and perhaps someday this significant divine union will be more fully expressed in our worship. Until that day, those who live out the Paschal Mysteries while attending the Remembrance of the Lord's Last Supper will bridge it to the First Supper in their personal devotion and their hearts.

The Last Supper was a Seder remembrance of the Exodus from Egypt's slavery and a new covenant meal of God's people. The early disciples simply called such remembrance meals "the breaking of the bread." While over the centuries the symbol of the cross became the preeminent sign of Christianity, perhaps a symbol more at the heart of the Christian experience would be a cup and a loaf of bread, or a table encircled by people. The Last Supper is the Lord's liberation banquet — "the breaking of the bread" that reflects a breaking out from the slavery of death, a breaking of all chains of enslavement to evil and of submission to imperial and religious powers.

The presence of the Risen Christ — who has poured himself out into all creation, transforming all creatures — makes this first meal of the Resurrected One a cosmic meal. It symbolizes the inclusion of all guests at this Easter breaking of the bread. It marks the breaking down of all barriers of race, sexuality and sexual orientation, all social classes and divisions, and the joyous breaking out of love and peace in a world dominated by greed and war. The Divine Spirit of Communion that is dynamically present and active in this Eucharistic meal glues together those who have been broken apart. This communion with Christ is also a communion with the Holy Spirit, who inspires all true communicants to become prophetic agents of change in the world. The bread transformed and infused by the Holy Spirit is then broken and shared in our lives, making us, and the world, the Body of Christ. The food of the new supper of Christ is the gift of the Body of the Risen One, who fills the universe in all its billions of galaxies.

The First Supper Prayer

First Supper of the Risen Christ,
  infuse yourself in every Eucharist
  so as to fill all who share that meal
  with love, courage and the promise
  that seals them with eternal life.

Faithfully for millenniums on end,
  the Risen Christ is seated at all meals
  where everyone is welcome to feast on
  a menu of love and acceptance,
  equality, peaceful pardon and forgiveness.

Faithful forever to his promise,
  even if only two are gathered
  in his name, in love, in peace,
  Christ is the invisible third
  present in every breaking of the bread.

At all of our common meals
  grant to us Easter eyes and hearts
  to be aware of the living presence
  of the Risen Lord of Easter.
May we be ever ready to accept
  our open invitation to share with Christ
  in God's great endless feast of life.

+

Let me take up my cross and follow you, Lord Jesus,
for by so doing I share in the liberation of the world.

Pilgrimage Instructions

We now leave this Upper Room, still dangerously radioactive with the presence of the Holy Spirit, and descend the stairs to the street level (*see map on page 55*). Turning left, we follow the road through the Zion Gate toward St. James Cathedral and the Citadel. Reaching the Citadel, we again turn left and depart from the Holy City through the Jaffa Gate. You will recognize this as the very place to which we came on the first day of our pilgrimage. To return to the beginning of our pilgrimage after all these days could lead you to believe that the Way is now completed. It is not. We still have two stations on our pilgrimage along the Via Gaudioso: the Nineteenth on Good Friday and Station Twenty on Holy Saturday.

Departing through the Jaffa Gate

THE NINETEENTH STATION

THE CROSSROAD OF EASTER SUPPERS

We praise you and we worship you, O Christ,
because by our crosses united, we redeem the world.

Scripture for the Nineteenth Station, the Emmaus Story

As they (the two disciples and the stranger) approached the village to which they were going, he gave the impression that he was going on farther. But they urged him, "Stay with us, for it is nearly evening." So he went in to stay with them. And it happened that, while he was with them at table, he took bread, said the blessing, broke the bread and gave it to them. With that their eyes were opened and they recognized him, but he vanished from their sight. They said to each other, "Were not our hearts burning within us as he spoke to us on the way and opened the scriptures to us?" They set out at once and returned to Jerusalem, where they found gathered the eleven and those with them.... Then the two recounted what had taken place on the way and how Christ was made known to them in the breaking of the bread.

—Luke 24: 28-35

On this most somber day, you may wish to revisit the Fifteenth Station, the Thursday and Friday of the fifth week in Lent. On this Good Friday as we recall the sorrowful station of the Cross of Calvary, we also reflect on why this day is called *good* as we stop to pray at the joyful station of the Crossroad. The village to which Luke refers is called Emmaus, which may correspond to the present-day village of Amwa, located about nineteen miles north of Jerusalem, or perhaps to el Qubeibeh, only eleven miles away from this Jaffa Gate. Also, the Crusaders built a church dedicated to the Emmaus meal at AbuGosh, eight miles from Jerusalem. In Luke's story the two disciples were able to return to the Holy City in one day, making el Qubeibeh or AbuGosh a more likely site. Leaving the tall walls of the Old City behind (*see map on page 20*), we walk down the Jaffa Road until it becomes the Ben Gurion Road. This was the same highway we took to Jerusalem after arriving from the Tel Aviv airport. Instead of walking the entire eight miles to the village of AbuGosh, we will stop at the first crossroad to eat lunch. More important than being at the actual site of the Emmaus meal is the act of breaking bread together at a *crossroad*.

Like the other disciples on that third day after the execution of Jesus, the Emmaus disciples had lost hope of any true change in their world and were literally at a painful crossroad. Should they smother their hopes and surrender to the power of Religion and the might of the Empire? Should they look for a new prophetic reformer and teacher? Throughout history, Jesus' disciples have found themselves at similar painful crossroads. The agony of Good Friday paralyzes us without the perspective and personal presence of Emmaus, without tasting and seeing

CROSSROADS EUCHARIST

the Risen Christ and having our hearts opened to a God's-eye understanding. It is through the sacramental presence of an Emmaus experience that Christ's disciples in every age and place have broken through the deadlock of their personal crossroads to find renewed hope and meaning.

Our word "sacrament" has its roots in *sacramentum*, "the pledge" or oath taken by a Roman soldier upon entering military service. The marking of the forehead with a cross in baptism speaks of *sacrament* in the old Roman military meaning of the word. Sometimes the army oath included branding the arm of a new recruit with a symbol of the general he was pledged to serve. In the same way, Christian baptismal recruits are branded with the Sign of the Cross, indelibly visible only to God. The Greek *mysterion* — "mystery" — which was originally used for sacramental manifestations of the power and love of God, expressed the invisible or hidden nature of sacred actions. The water of your baptism was a visible sign of the invisible *mysterion* by which you were incorporated into the death and resurrection of Jesus. To be baptized is to become a perpetual liturgist, a celebrant of all of life as a sacrament of God's love and power. Jesus' death was such a sacred doorway into the Reign of God, where God is the *Mysterion*, the hidden reality shaping and sharing in our meals, our loves, our joys, sorrows, sickness and death.

It is significant that the disciples pressed *a stranger* — not a recognizable form of their Galilean friend Jesus or some haloed, glorious Risen Christ — to remain and share supper with them. Every gospel sacrament, like the Emmaus sacrament of hospitality, is a door into the Kingdom of God. To enter through any of these mysterious doors with which life is crowded is to enter into the presence of the Risen Christ. It is a living sacrament, not a dead religion, that enables us to break out of our boxed-in, dead-end ways of thinking and being. So, first of all, the appearance of the Risen Lord at the roadside of this Nineteenth Station reaffirms the liberation of the Divine Presence from imprisonment in the tabernacles of temples and churches into a living, breathing sacrament of love. It continues yesterday's station, which celebrated the Easter gift of the Holy Spirit consecrating not only all creation but all human acts into sacraments of the Spirit.

In the sacraments of the church, as well as in all gospel sacraments like Emmaus, the divine presence is hidden from natural eyes. This Crossroad Station of the Triumphant Cross is but the first of a hundred million eucharists, spelled with a small "e." The Lord's Supper, of course, is called the Eucharist — Greek for "Thanksgiving" — and is spelled with a capital "E." It is a corporate, public act of worship that is ritualized with precisely defined rules and rubrics. The millions of little "e" eucharists require only that we observe the rubrics of Emmaus: welcome, generous sharing, a table open even to strangers, and a passionate desire to share food and life by breaking bread together. The Emmaus sacrament is a revelation into the many other gospel sacraments, among which are care of the poor, clothing the naked, visiting the imprisoned, comforting the sorrowing, and providing hospitality to the stranger. For disciples of the Spirit, all of life is a sacramental door through which all our daily activities can become holy intersections, Triumphant Crossroads where God and humans come together.

Only three were present at that roadside supper of Emmaus. Only twelve — and perhaps a few more — were present at the Last Supper in the Upper Room. These facts are significant, for they reveal that if our hearts are to burn with love and delight in the presence of the Risen One, we must have firsthand, intimate experiences. Untiring, joyful, energetic discipleship is not possible for secondhand disciples who have only third- or fourth-hand experiences of faith. The Emmaus experience is a pattern of the personal, direct sacramental contacts that the Risen Christ intends for every disciple. The kind of touchable experience desired by the doubting disciple Thomas is both normal and necessary for all of us who follow Christ. We should seek tangible, firsthand fulfillments of the words of Jesus that "whatever you do to the least of my brethren, even to those who are not known as disciples, you do to me: I was a stranger and you welcomed me, hungry and you gave me food..." (see Matthew 25: 35-40). Every hidden Easter appearance of the Divine Mystery present in an act of kindness can create a faith-ignited blaze in our hearts.

In his Last Supper farewell, Jesus promised that he would be with us always. The Risen Promise-Keeper is daily in your midst. Train your eyes to see with an Easter vision so your faith can be enflamed. And rejoice that such Emmaus opportunities abound everywhere along the roadway of your daily life.

+

Let me take up my cross and follow you, Lord Jesus,
for by so doing I share in the liberation of the world.

Pilgrimage Instructions

To reach our Twentieth and final Station on our Pilgrimage Way of the Cross, we leave this Station of the Emmaus Meal and return up Ben Gurion Road and the old Jaffa Road leading to the Old City of Jerusalem. The Holy City has many additional sacred places we could visit — not to mention those in Bethlehem and in Galilee to the north — but our destination is the site of the Ascension of the Risen Christ on the Mount of Olives. Upon reaching the Jaffa Gate (*see map on page 55*), once again we turn to the right and follow the familiar road that winds past Mt. Zion and the southern walls of the Old City toward the Mount of Olives (*see map on page 51*).

Crossing the Kidron Valley, we continue up past the silver-leafed olive groves on the road to Bethphage. Before reaching the Church of the Pater Noster, there is a road on the left that leads to the Mosque of the Ascension, which was once the Church of the Ascension. Through the trees we can see a small Muslim minaret, or prayer tower, indicating that the area is Muslim property. Across the valley under the golden Dome of the Mosque of the Rock is the sacrificial stone of Abraham from which the Prophet Muhammad ascended into heaven on his crucial Night Journey. Muslims recognize Jesus as an important prophet, second only to Muhammad. They also reverence this site of the ascension of Christ, saying, "for did not Muhammad himself depart this world in similar fashion?"

Sacred to both Muslims and Christians, the Mosque of the Ascension is a small medieval chapel on the proposed spot of Christ's Ascension. Now part of a larger mosque enclosure, this octagonal-shaped building has a stone dome, its walls still marked by small marble Crusader columns. Again, like those sites visited inside the Holy Sepulcher, a very significant sacred event that occurred outside in nature is now enclosed with four (or, in this case, eight) walls and a roof. As prayerful as the inside of the church-mosque is, we go outside, under the blue dome of the sky, to pray on this hill covered with olive trees and to ponder the Risen Christ's Ascension into heaven.

THE FORTIETH AND LAST DAY OF THE PILGRIMAGE
Holy Saturday, the Eve of Easter

THE TWENTIETH STATION
THE FINAL ASCENSION OF CHRIST

We praise you and we follow you, O Christ,
because by our crosses united, we redeem the world.

Scriptures for the Twentieth Station

He then led them out near Bethany, and with hands upraised, blessed them. As he blessed them, he parted from them and was taken up to heaven. —Luke 24: 50-51

As the eleven were at table, he (the Risen Christ) appeared to them and rebuked them for their unbelief and hardness of heart...and he said to them, "Go into the whole world and proclaim the good news to all creation. The one who believes and accepts baptism will be saved (liberated)...." Then, after speaking to them, the Lord Jesus was taken

up into heaven.... But they went forth and preached everywhere,
while the Lord worked with them. —Mark 16: 14-16, 19-20

The eleven went to Galilee, to the mountain to which Jesus had ordered
them, and when they saw him they worshiped, but doubted. Jesus
approached and said to them, "Go, therefore and make disciples of all
nations, baptizing them in the name of the Father, and of the Son,
and of the Holy Spirit.... And behold, I am with you always, until the
end of the age." —Matthew 28: 16-20

Holy Saturday, traditionally a day of waiting and prayer, is an
apt time for faithful followers of the Risen Christ to reflect on
the Ascension, for it is a feast still waiting to unfold fully. The
Gospel of John does not record the Ascension, and Matthew
alludes to it happening on some unnamed mountain in Galilee
where the Risen Jesus promises to be with us until the end of
the age. Interestingly, Mark places the Ascension at a table
where the eleven apostles were gathered for a meal, with the
implication that this table was in the Upper Room. Our
pilgrimage has chosen the geography of Luke, who places the
site of the Ascension here at Bethany on the Mount of Olives.
Yet, again, rather than the actual location of the event, it is the
Ascension itself that is most significant.

The heavens, by global consent, have ever been considered
to be the home of the gods and of God. And ascending was a
common feat for heroes in the mythic world of the ancient
Greeks and Romans. Emperors and heroic figures were often
taken up into the heavens to become gods. Even in the biblical
tradition, the taking up of the Hebrew heroes Enoch and Elijah
into heaven was a sign of divine approval. For the shamefully
crucified Jesus, the Ascension was the ultimate sign of God's
affirmation of his selfless way of life and death, raising him
infinitely high above his enemies.

Both Mark and Luke used the words "taken up" for the

ascending of Christ. They parallel the passive voice of the angels' words at his tomb, "He has been raised," both implying actions happening to a person. These two passive expressions make a significant spiritual and theological distinction. They suggest that the Risen Jesus is the first of all those whom the Spirit of God will raise up as full shareholders in the victory of

"His face became as dazzling as the sun, his clothing as radiant as light." –Matthew 17: 2

Christ. It was Love that refused to allow the Beloved to cease to exist and raised him out of the tomb. Now, that same Love seeking total union magnetically draws him back again to his Beloved.

That magnetic power of attraction, as well as Jesus' final words in Matthew's Gospel, suggests a fresh understanding of the Ascension. Unlike believers of the distant past, we do not think of God's dwelling as being exclusively up in the heavens. Not only was it Christ's mission to be Emmanuel, God among us, but his departing words as he was ascending into heaven were, "Behold, I am with you always, until the end of the age." So perhaps an equally appropriate term for the Ascension of Christ would be the Assimilation. Though Jesus was going heavenward to be with the Father, he was also going to be fully and ever present on the earth. After his disciples' numerous experiences of his risen, living presence among them, now the Risen Ascending Christ is assimilated into all creation, just as food is transformed and absorbed as living tissue. Mark's table Ascension is an appropriate setting, suggesting that the Risen Jesus, as the Bread of Life, would be assimilated, like food and drink, into all of life. His Ascension instruction to his disciples was, "proclaim the good news to all creation" — be agents of assimilation, leaven for the Bread of Life to become the fabric of, and thus to transform, all of creation.

The Ascension-Assimilation, then, is the finale of Jesus' earthy physical presence, the final act in which God bestows upon him a cosmic glory in inverse proportion to the abject shame of the crucifixion. Besides being the grand finale, it is also the overture to the gospel of the Spirit. The Divine Mystery delights in composing infinite overtures of new beginnings. These overtures are ever conducted by the Spirit, who endlessly and freshly unfolds a newness of life that emerges from both the Source and the Son. The threefold community of the Father, Son and Holy Spirit gives birth to the ever-flowing Water

People of God as the always-new community of the Risen Jesus. Those who are Breath-born by the Spirit are ordained to be generators of new life. And because the newness and fresh change of these very divine invasions are as frightening to religion and the social order as they were in Jesus' time, the Risen Lord pledges not only his abiding presence but also that, in the words of Mark, he will "work with" us.

The Ascending One's farewell words on this Mount of Olives are a holy Declaration of Independence from holy cities: "Go into the whole world!" Go forth from this Holy City of Jerusalem and make every city, village and hamlet you enter holy. After you deliver the gift of the good news, may all who receive it be in awe that the soil beneath their feet is holy land. Be my living words to all creatures, wild and tame, for all of creation shares in my resurrection along with humanity.

It is appropriate that his Declaration of Independence for all creation was proclaimed on this lush, green mountain under the cobalt-blue dome of the sky. His message is still conveyed by the wind rustling the leaves of olive trees and by the joyful songs of birds as well as by his faithful followers.

The Intoxicating Gospel of the Spirit

As the Risen Jesus was about to be taken up into God, his voice carried outward beyond the eleven disciples gathered on this hillside to reach his disciples of every age: Go forth carrying your new wine skins, intoxicated on the new wine of God's rich vintage. Beware of trying to pour this new wine into old wineskins, into old structures and institutions. As I once said, "No one puts new wine in old wineskins. If he does, the wine will burst the skins, and the wine will be lost along with the skins. No, my new wine demands new skins" (Mark 2: 22). As disciples of my Spirit keep your wineskins fresh and flexible, and constantly create new wineskins for this intoxicating vintage of God.

Go forth from here in all directions across the world as

grapevine branches of me, the Divine Vine. Each of your global branches is pulsing with my abundant life, for the vital sap of the Spirit flows through you when you are intimately connected with me. Go and bear abundant fruit in whatever place you find yourselves. As I once said, "It is the glory of my Father that you should bear fruit.... I commission you to go out and to bear fruit that will endure" (John 15: 8, 16). Do not be anxious or fearful when your grand church buildings finally crumble into dust, your religious orders and pious organizations rise and then fall, for it is *you*, and not the structures, who are to bear fruit that will endure. Be zealous, then, to cultivate the durable fruits of love, reconciliation and peace, and strive to change the hearts of others by first changing your own heart.

Go forth and bear a harvest of good fruit that yields a hundredfold in every corner of your world. My death on the cross was a political and social act. So, as my extensions, you must influence your whole world until it fully reflects God's kingdom, where all people will experience justice and the abundance of good things. You are to continue my cosmic work of redemption by transforming the worlds of politics and business, art and education, medicine and entertainment — and not simply attempting to "save" individual souls! Labor tirelessly to change social structures from the outside in as well as the inside out. Work to change the laws and structures of your community and your nation so as to liberate those who are imprisoned by poverty, substandard education and violence, and by discriminating laws and social attitudes.

Disciples of my Spirit, I send you forth from this Mount of Olives as cross-carrying revolutionaries in the pattern of my life. Do not be afraid; for the message I once received in Nazareth, I now say to you:

> *The Spirit of the Lord is upon you*
> *because the Spirit has anointed you*
> *to bring glad tidings to the poor.*

That Spirit has sent you to proclaim liberty to prisoners
and recovery of sight to the blind,
to let the oppressed go free,
and to proclaim a Jubilee Year acceptable to the Lord.

—Luke 4: 18-19

The same Spirit that anointed me has, in your baptism,

also anointed each of you to be Jubilee messengers of God's pardon for all debts, joyful broadcasters of the release of all held captive. Go forth now, but not in peace! Depart from here aflame in the Spirit. As you go out into the world, do not sorrowfully drag your crosses; raise them up high! Do not carry your crosses; live them courageously, especially your crosses of conviction and commitment, your crosses of revolution and change, your crosses of self-sacrifice and love. Let your crosses be covert emblems of being an Easter people. May they be indelible labels of authentic lovers and infallible insignias of mystical followers. For it is by these crosses that you and I together continue to redeem and liberate the world.

+

Let me take up my cross and go out into the world, Lord Jesus, for by so doing I share in the liberation of the world.

HOLY LAND SOUVENIRS

With the completion of our forty-day pilgrimage, it is time to depart from the Holy Land. Pilgrims usually desire to return home with some Holy Land souvenir from their visit: perhaps a holy image, a rosary or cross made of olive wood, or a small pebble from some sacred site. The most excellent souvenir of this pilgrimage, however, is an inner life altered and energized by having come into contact with holy places still radioactive with the Divine Presence. By prayer and reflection you have been able to experience — maybe even more than those who actually

travel to the Holy Land — the mysterious power of the Way of the Cross. Courageous pilgrims who expose their hearts to the sufferings and joys of the Risen Jesus on his Baptismal Way never return home the same persons as those who departed.

The same is true of those who enter the mysterious water birth of Baptism. In the early days of the community of the Risen Jesus, and even today, those who experience his baptismal dying rise up as radically new persons. True converts of the Spirit are always authentically changed — provided their intention is to undergo a genuine conversion in life. So, whether you are preparing to experience this great sacrament or have used this pilgrimage as a rededication of your infant or adult baptism, I pray that the souvenir you bring back from these forty days is an awakened desire to live as a new person in Christ: more liberated, more compassionate, and more deeply alive and loving.

Tomorrow is the Feast of Easter. This feast of joy once signaled the time to abandon the penances and crosses of the past forty days. Instead, as a pilgrim of the Holy Land, celebrate this Easter with a joyful gratitude for the chosen gift of your unique cross. Express the transforming grace of your gift by lifting it high as the glorious instrument of victory and liberation for yourself and for the world.

APPENDIX

THE DOME OF THE ROCK

The large natural rock formation located directly under the Dome of the Rock is generally believed to be the top of Mount Moriah, upon which Abraham prepared to sacrifice his son Isaac and on which Solomon's Temple was built around B.C. 950. It was destroyed in 585 B.C. by the Babylonians, who carried off the Ark of the Covenant from inside the Temple's Holy of Holies. King Herod began rebuilding the Temple in B.C. 20, including the construction of the huge earthen platform of the present Temple Mount. With the Ark of the Covenant now lost, the Holy of Holies in this new temple was an empty room in which God dwelled. The precise location of this Holy of Holies on the Mount is not certain, and the Roman Army destroyed it along with the entire city of Jerusalem in A.D. 70.

The Prophet Muhammad is said to have left the earth from this stone on his famous Night Journey. This was one of the key events in the life of the Prophet: He was carried from Mecca to Jerusalem, and from this rock he made the *Miraaj*, the ascent through the heavens to God's presence, returning to Mecca in the morning. Upon the site of the ruins of Herod's Temple, the Muslim Caliph Abd el-Malik constructed the magnificent Dome of the Rock in A.D. 691. After shrines in Mecca and Medina, this mosque of the *Haram Esh-Sharif*, the Noble Sanctuary, is the third holiest site of Islam. Locating it on such a significant spot in Jerusalem also appears to be a symbolic statement that the new religion of Islam was now the successor and supplanter of both Judaism and Christianity. The brilliant golden dome of this mosque was originally made with copper but was covered with gold leaf by the late King Hussein of Jordan.

Near the center of the Haram Esh-Sharif on the eastern side of the Dome of the Rock is the smaller Dome of the Chain, a site commonly considered to be the center of the world. A long chain once hung from this splendid mosaic dome. Legend holds that whoever told a lie while holding this chain would be struck dead by lightning.

Extremists among both Orthodox Jews and Fundamentalist Christians await the Coming of the Messianic Age that promises the building of a New Temple on this very site. Despite the fact that the Israelis captured the entire city in 1967, the Temple Mount continues to be the property of a Muslim religious foundation, and as long as they retain control of this ancient holy site, any future Messianic Temple is not a possibility.

THE PROPHET MUHAMMAD

The Prophet Muhammad, the founder of Islam, was born in the Arabian city of Mecca in A.D. 570. It is said that around the age of 40 he began to receive divine revelations from Allah, the One God. These revelations were collected in print in the Quran, the holy book of Islam. Muhammad's preaching that there was only one God was not warmly received among Arabic peoples, who worshiped many gods, and in 622 he was forced to flee to Medina. His religion of Islam, meaning surrender to

Allah, spread quickly. He died in 632, and within four years the militant armies of his devoted followers had come thundering out of the Arabian desert and conquered the Holy Land.

THE MOSQUE

Friday is the weekly day of worship for Muslims, a day when all devout men go to the mosque or prayer hall. Because the religious life of Muslims follows the lunar calendar, the dome or tower of a mosque is crowned with the symbol of a crescent-shaped moon. The mosque traditionally has a dome over the prayer hall with a platform on one side from which the *iman*, the religious teacher and spiritual leader, delivers the Friday sermon.

The prayer hall, like a synagogue, is completely bare of art images, in fidelity to their scriptural prohibition. However, mosques are frequently decorated with beautiful, artistic mosaic tile work, featuring creative calligraphy of texts from the Quran. Also, the floors of major mosques are covered with elaborately colorful Persian rugs. Next to the mosque is a tower called a minaret, with a balcony from which a *muezzin*, a crier, intones the five daily calls to prayer. These ritual prayers are recited while kneeling in the direction of Mecca. Today's pilgrims and visitors to Jerusalem, as elsewhere in the Islamic world, hear these calls to prayer from a recorded cassette that is broadcast over loudspeakers.

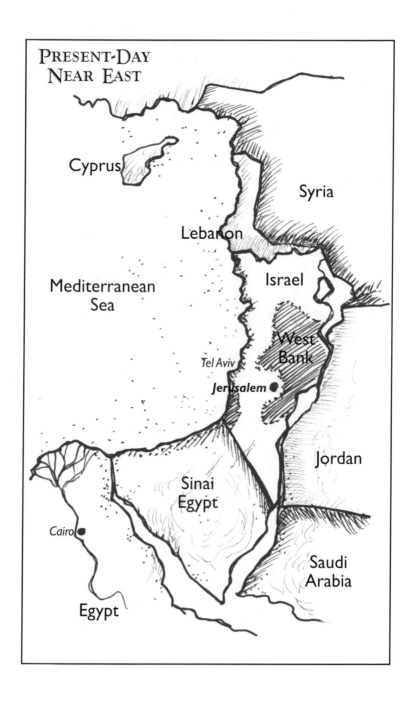

PRESENT-DAY
NEAR EAST

Cyprus

Syria

Lebanon

Mediterranean
Sea

Israel

West
Bank

Tel Aviv

Jerusalem

Jordan

Sinai
Egypt

Cairo

Saudi
Arabia

Egypt

ISRAEL-PALESTINE:
A *PROMISED* OR A *POISONED* LAND?

Over fifty years ago the English writer G.K. Chesterton wrote, "Jerusalem is a small town of big things...all the most important and interesting powers in history are here gathered within the area of a quiet village; and if they are not always friends, at least they are necessarily neighbors." He continued with his impressions about visiting there: "I felt almost a momentary impulse to flee the place, like one who has received an omen. For two voices had met in my ears; and within the same narrow space and in the same dark hour, electric and yet eclipsed with cloud, I had heard Islam crying from the turret and Israel wailing at the wall." It is not unusual for present-day pilgrims to Palestine-Israel to feel a similar ambivalence. While this land is the holiest of ground, it is also often a battleground — and pilgrims can easily get caught in the cross fire.

In fact, at the time of the printing of this book, few pilgrims are visiting the Holy Land and the Holy City because of the deep unrest in the region and the ever-present danger of terrorist bombings. Many Christians committed to justice and peace are refusing to visit Israel as a statement of protest against what is almost universally regarded as that nation's unjust treatment of the Palestinian people, and Israel's tourist economy is suffering as a result. Archbishop Desmond Tutu has called the present situation in Israel "Apartheid in the Holy Land." As South Africa was boycotted because of its practice of apartheid, so now Israel is experiencing similar treatment by much of the rest of the world.

The atmosphere of oppression and terrorism is not new to the Holy Land. The intense hatred and violence that exists today in Israel-Palestine in some ways parallels the conditions that existed at the time of Jesus' trial and crucifixion-execution in Jerusalem. Indeed, first-century Israel also suffered from the violence of terrorism, only the terrorists were Jews who were striking out at the oppressive rule of Rome. Some of these terrorists were members of a fanatical liberation group called the *Zealots*, who were opposed to the Roman occupation, and at least one Zealot was a disciple of Jesus. The Romans called a more violent Jewish terrorist group *Sicarri*, "stabbers," because they concealed daggers beneath their garments. Like militant Palestinian bombers of today, they chose crowded public areas to strike their blows for the liberation of their land occupied by foreigners. In Jesus' trial, the charge presented to Pilate by the Temple hierarchy was that Jesus wanted to be the Jewish King and to restore Jewish independence. Today, as then, in the tiny narrow strip of land between the Jordan River and the Mediterranean Sea, political and religious forces have sought to preserve the status quo even by violent means.

A Brief History of the Promised Land

Because of its strategic location at the intersection of routes connecting three continents, Palestine has not only been a meeting place of cultural and religious influences, it has also been a magnet for conflict and conquest. The Canaanites were the first inhabitants of the region in recorded history (during the Bronze Age, between 3500 and 1500 B.C.). The land of Canaan saw waves of ethnically diverse invaders, including the Amorites, Hittites, Hurians and Egyptians.

A century or so after the Philistines (from whom the name Palestine comes) conquered parts of Canaan, the Hebrews returned to the land of their forefathers Abraham, Isaac and Jacob. Released from slavery and having wandered for years in the Sinai Desert, the Jews crossed over the Jordan around the year 1200 B.C. and under the leadership of Joshua "put to the sword all living creatures in the city of Jericho: men and women, young and old, as well as oxen, sheep and asses" (Joshua 6: 21).

Following generations of warring against the Philistines, King David captured Jerusalem around 1000 B.C. and made it his capital. Fifty years later his son King Solomon built the first Jewish Temple on Mount Moriah, and the Jewish nation flourished under his rule. After Solomon's death, however, the kingdom was divided into Israel in the north and Judah in the south. In 722 B.C. Israel was conquered by the Assyrians, and in 586 B.C. Judah, including Jerusalem, was overrun by the Babylonians, who destroyed Solomon's Temple and exiled the Jews to Babylon.

When Persia conquered the Babylonian Empire fifty years later, King Cyrus the Great permitted the Jews to return to Judah and rebuild Jerusalem. But in 333 B.C. Alexander the Great marched through the region, and it remained under Greek rule until the Maccabees, Jewish freedom fighters, successfully revolted in the mid-second century B.C. and set up an independent state. This lasted only a short time, however, when in 63 B.C., Jerusalem was overcome by Rome, who appointed Herod as King of Judea. Then, a generation after Jesus' death, a failed revolt in 70 A.D. prompted the Romans to destroy Herod's Temple and the entire city of Jerusalem.

In 315 A.D. the Roman Emperor Constantine ended the persecution of Christians with a decree of religious tolerance for Christian and pagan religions. This marked the beginning of Christians making pilgrimages to the Holy Land, and many pilgrims remained to build churches and monasteries. In 614 A.D. the Persians invaded Palestine, massacring the Christians and destroying their shrines. Then in 638 the army of the Muslim Caliph Omar conquered the land, and Muslims became the new rulers. Omar permitted both Christians and Jews to visit and live in Jerusalem provided they paid an "infidels' tax."

In 1009 a new Muslim ruler launched a violent persecution of all non-Muslims and destroyed the Church of the Holy Sepulcher. Christian Europe responded with the

Crusades, and the next two hundred years in the Holy Land was filled with wars and bloodshed. When the last Crusade ended in 1270, the Holy Land was under the control of the Muslim Mameluks. Then the Ottoman Turks swept through Palestine in 1517 and ruled, with brief violent interruptions, for several hundred years. During World War I the Ottoman Empire chose to become an ally of Germany and was defeated in Palestine by Great Britain and her allies in 1917.

1917 to 1948

For thirty years following World War I, Palestine was under the control of the British, who in different agreements promised the Arabs independence for their countries and the Jews a "national homeland" in Palestine. Anti-Semitism in Europe at this time had given rise to the Zionist movement, which promoted the creation of a Jewish State in Palestine with the slogan, "A land without people for a people without a land." Yet Palestine was not a land without people; there were around 500,000 resident Arabs, some of whom traced their lineage back to the Canaanites, compared to about 85,000 resident Jews.

The increasing Jewish immigration from Europe during the next twenty years caused friction between Jews and the Arab inhabitants, with both sides engaging in ever-escalating acts of terrorism.

In an attempt to reduce tension, the British established a law limiting Jewish immigration, which only inspired attacks on the British by Jewish terrorists. In one incident a Jewish bomb exploded in the King David Hotel, the site of the British Military and Colonial headquarters, killing eighty British and wounding hundreds more. As the terrorism and violence by both Jews and Arabs escalated, so did the number of Jewish immigrants from Europe. When the horrors of the Holocaust during World War II produced world sympathy for European Jews, Zionism was also more favorably received. And although Britain restricted the number of Jewish immigrants, many Jews found their way to Palestine illegally.

Unable to control the land, the British strongly supported the United Nations resolution of November 29, 1947, which would partition Palestine into Jewish and Arab nations. In this UN proposal, Jerusalem was to be an international city or zone belonging to all peoples — Jews, Muslims and Christians (see map on page 235). The surrounding Arab nations refused to accept the creation of a Jewish State in what they considered land stolen from Arab Palestinians. They attacked the newly created Israel in the War of 1948, but under David Ben-Gurion, the well-trained Israeli army, outnumbered by two to one, defeated the disorganized Arabs. As a result of the Israeli victory, some 500,000 to 750,000 refugees fled to neighboring Arab countries. The Jews owned 7% of Palestine at the beginning of 1948, and after the war they controlled 80%, with Jerusalem a city divided between Arabs and Jews.

In 1949 Israel passed the Law of Return, which extended to all Jews anywhere in the world the right to live as citizens in Israel. The continuously increasing Jewish population required

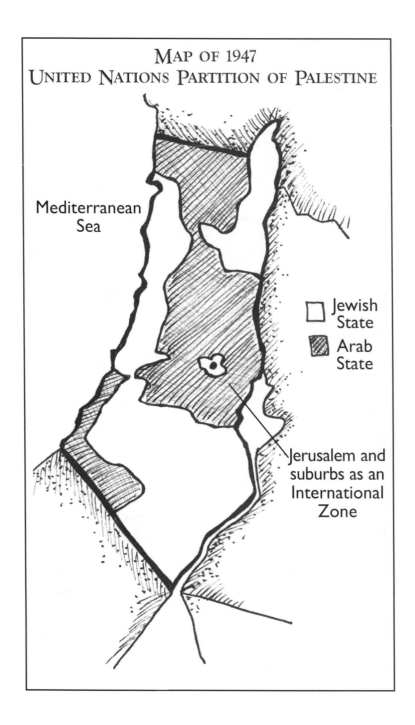

MAP OF 1947
UNITED NATIONS PARTITION OF PALESTINE

Mediterranean
Sea

☐ Jewish
State

▨ Arab
State

Jerusalem and
suburbs as an
International
Zone

more and more land to house the new immigrants. In 1967 Israel launched a preemptive attack on Egyptian forces gathering in the Sinai and in six short days defeated the Arab forces. The Israelis now occupied all of the remaining Palestinian land, including the West Bank, Sinai, Gaza and the Golan Heights, as well as the entire city of Jerusalem. At this time they began their construction of Jewish settlements in the occupied Palestinian land. Another brief war in 1973 saw no change in these 1967 boundaries.

In 1987 the Palestinians, weary of Israeli occupation and fearful that any negotiated resolution would be slanted in favor of the Jews, began the *Intifada* (the shaking off). In this grassroots revolt against Israeli occupation of their homeland, Palestinian boys, armed only with rocks, battled Israel's tanks and armed military. Increasingly frustrated at the turning of this millennium, the *Intifada* exchanged stones for human bombs. They targeted Israeli citizens as well as Jewish settlers living in the Occupied Territories. Israel responded with assassinations of over seventy Palestine Liberation Organization officials and many forms of brutal retaliation by the Israeli army.

Religion and the Holy Land

Its location on the Eastern end of the Mediterranean Sea, along trade routes linking Asia, Africa and Europe, has made Palestine-Israel a strategic and political prize for many invaders, from the early ferocious and fearsome Amorites and Hittites to the often ruthless expansionist empires of the Egyptians, Assyrians, Babylonians, Greeks and Romans. However, much of the blood that has stained the Holy Land throughout its history has been due to religious reasons.

Indeed, the land's history is steeped in religion. Jerusalem, particularly, has been considered a holy place from antiquity, when on the small mountain later to be called Moriah early inhabitants created a shrine to their local god *Shalem* (whose memory still lingers in the name Jerusalem). The Canaanites later converted it into a holy shrine to their god Baal. We have already seen how this was the site of the covenant God made with Abraham and his people forever (Abraham being the Father of Faith to Muslims and Christians as well as Jews). That same piece of land was also the site of Israel's great Temples, the place of Muhammad's *Miraaj* or Night Journey, his Ascension into heaven — marked by the famous Dome of the Rock Mosque that still towers over the Jerusalem landscape — and the location of many significant events in the redemptive ministry of Jesus and his apostles. The many mosques, churches, shrines and other holy structures in and around Jerusalem are firsthand markers of the core faith experiences of Judaism, Christianity and Islam. Israel-Palestine is the spiritual homeland to all three great religions. And just as both Israelis and Palestinians believe they have legitimate political claims on the land, they both legitimately believe Jerusalem to be their own true spiritual capital from the beginning of time.

Because of this intertwining of spiritual roots and because of the many strong challenges made against each of these faiths over the ages, it is not surprising that this holy ground should become a battleground. Indeed, each religion has believed that the land has been consecrated in part by the blood that has been spilt there because of religious conviction. For example, when the Greeks repressed Jewish religious practice in the second century B.C., the Maccabees courageously lived out their willingness to die rather than compromise their faith. In Jesus' time, the Zealots, who had more political than spiritual aspirations, similarly stood up to the Romans. And, of course, Christians consider Jesus' blood shed in Jerusalem to be the holiest of acts, summing up all the sacrifices in Jewish worship and the lives of the prophets.

Moreover, as the early Church Father Tertullian suggested, "the blood of martyrs is the seed of the Church." Christianity was consecrated and spread through the Roman world in large measure due to the shedding of martyrs' innocent blood in the pattern of Christ's crucifixion. As we have seen in the course of this book, Stephen, James and other martyrs in Jerusalem were among the earliest and most significant in the Christian tradition. The prayer among contemporary Palestinians to "be given the honor of being one of the martyrs in Jerusalem" echoes the call of early Christianity.

However, just as it was in Jesus' day, religion can be misdirected, fanaticized or abused — used to advance personal or political interests at the expense of justice, peace or any vestiges of love. For example, while there was much good intent in the Crusades, much of the enterprise went awry as armies went off to battle amid the cry, "God wills it!" In the 1099 campaign, the Crusader armies captured Jerusalem in a massive slaughter of Muslims and Jews. One crusader wrote of the battle on the Temple Mount: "Men rode in blood up to their knees and bridle reins. Indeed, it was a just and splendorous judgment of God." In every religion and in every age, "holy wars" have been perpetuated, and Scriptures, like the passage from Joshua quoted on page 230, have regretfully been used historically to justify the grossest discrimination against those who are not of "our" religion. The person of God, under a variety of names, has been used to justify "death to infidels" — the slaughter of innocent individuals and even mass ethnic cleansing.

"For you are a people sacred to the Lord, your God, who has chosen you from all the nations of the earth to be a people peculiarly his own" (Deuteronomy 7: 6). Misappropriating and exclusively interpreting such holy words can be lethal and toxic to the heart of real religion. Claims to be God's exclusively Chosen People easily lead to an arrogance that invites violence, destruction, killing and war — a distortion based on the belief that "we" are divinely superior to other nations. Of course, claiming to be a superior people is not restricted to the Jewish nation. The ancient Romans boasted, *Civis Romanus sum*, "I am a Roman Citizen," a unique status making them superior to others, a belief that gave them license to conquer and enslave others by military might. The twentieth century vividly saw Adolph Hitler bestow upon the German people the status of the Aryan people being the Master Race and under God's special care. In World War II, German soldiers wore belt buckles inscribed with *Gott Mit Uns*, "God is with us," reflecting the belief that regardless of their aggression, God was on their side.

We in the United States have at times been infected with this disease of thinking ourselves superior and under God's unique protection — at the expense of other people, including the original inhabitants of our land. While cultivating God's providence and even being patriotic are virtues, when we exclusively pray "God bless America," instead of "God bless the world," we too easily make the transition into believing "My country, right or wrong." The annihilation of non-Christian cultures by some missionaries shows, too, that Christians are not immune to this disease of superiority. Even the Second Vatican Council's adoption of the term "the People of God," once reserved for the Jewish people, can, if misunderstood, divorce the Catholic faithful from participating in God's Global Family of all peoples.

The Contemporary Conflict in the Promised Land

This long political and religious history can help us to understand not only the forces that fed into Jesus' crucifixion but also to appreciate something of the volatile contemporary circumstances in the Promised Land. Following the attack on the World Trade Center on September 11, 2001, Americans have become understandably appalled and frightened at the escalating terrorism that has much of its roots in Israel-Palestine. It is easy to take sides against those associated with terrorist acts, particular the Palestinians who promote suicide bombings and whose anger, hate and human bombs have taken innocent lives. However, before we too quickly rally around that pro-

Israeli position under a flag reading, "God is on our side," we need to reflect on whose side God really is. The book of Judith (appropriately, verse 9: 11) says: "For God is the God of the oppressed, the helper of the lowly, the avenger of the helpless, the protector of the contemptible, the savior of the desperate." Judith would suggest that if God does indeed take sides, God is on the side of the oppressed and powerless. Justice, therefore, calls us to look at the present situation in the Holy Land closely.

From the beginning of the existence of the state of Israel, its treatment of Palestinian people has been questionable, displacing countless Palestinians from their homes and land without anything resembling due process. The Gaza Strip has been called "the world's largest concentration camp," where 1,200,000 refugee Palestinians are lodged in 146 square miles of sandy, barren hills. Jewish settlers continue to build settlements there and now occupy 30% of Gaza in insulated communities guarded by Israeli military *(see map on page 241)*. In the West Bank alone since 1967 the Jewish State has constructed over 200 Jewish settlements. In recent reprisals against Palestinian resistance, they have engaged in a form of State terrorism, destroying thousands of groves of Palestinian olive trees and hundreds of precious water wells, while systematically bulldozing the homes of many Palestinians. The Jewish military has engaged in the deliberate destruction of the Palestinian economy, electrical works, water systems and roads, as well as destroying municipal, banking and school records. All along, they have targeted noncombatant civilians, under the pretext that these acts are necessary for the safeguarding of national security. Some international groups have labeled this excessive destruction as societal genocide.

American Jewish political scientist Edmund Hanauer has pointed out that more than 100 Israeli army reservists have refused to serve in Israeli-occupied Palestinian territories, stating that they will "fight no more to rule, deport, destroy, blockade,

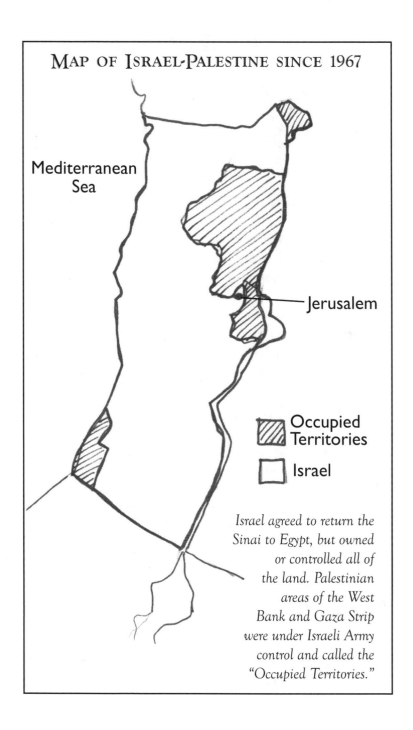

MAP OF ISRAEL-PALESTINE SINCE 1967

Mediterranean
Sea

——Jerusalem

Occupied
Territories

Israel

*Israel agreed to return the
Sinai to Egypt, but owned
or controlled all of
the land. Palestinian
areas of the West
Bank and Gaza Strip
were under Israeli Army
control and called the
"Occupied Territories."*

exterminate, starve and humiliate" the Palestinian people. Hanauer went on to say that "Israel's leading human rights group, B'Tselem, reports that Israel has violated 29 of the 30 Articles of the Universal Declaration of Human Rights.... B'Tselem also concluded that the experience of the 200,000 East Jerusalem Palestinians living under Israeli occupation has been 'a history of dispossession, systematic discrimination and a consistent assault' on their 'basic human rights.' " Furthermore, a declaration made by 1,110 American religious leaders in 1999 encouraged the United States government to reevaluate its $3 billion yearly foreign aid to Israel, citing that U.S. law prohibits foreign aid to countries "engaging in a consistent pattern of gross violations of internationally recognized human rights."

It is also critical to remember that Israel still refuses to acknowledge the mandate of United Nations Resolution 242. This resolution requires the return of all the land taken from the Palestinians in 1967 known as "the Occupied Territories" so that the refugees can return to their homes. Americans tend to be uninformed and misinformed about this bitter Near Eastern conflict, often suffering from "weak ears," the inability to filter out propaganda, be it from the State of Israel or the American government. It is interesting to note the scores of UN recommendations to sanction Israeli conduct in which the only dissenting vote among the fourteen nations on the Security Council has come from the United States.

Pure politics aside, religious leaders from around the world, including Pope John Paul II, Archbishop Desmond Tutu and Jerusalem's Catholic Patriarch Archbishop Michael Sabbah, have encouraged justice for the Palestinians and that, in the Pope's words, "relationships between all should be inspired by mutual respect, humility and trust." Archbishop Sabbah reminds us of the dangers of assuming exclusivist positions, saying "that every exclusivity or every human supremacy is against the prophetic character of Jerusalem...to be a city of peace and harmony among all who dwell therein." He also points out that the covenant God made with Abraham was with " 'the father of many nations' and a 'blessing for the nations of the earth'.... That is why Jews, Christians and Muslims today venerate together Abraham as their common 'father of faith' in the one God who blesses all people." Archbishop Tutu clearly presents the three options available to the State of Israel: (1) exterminate or remove all Palestinians, (2) maintain the present high-tension stalemated situation, or (3) strive for a peace based on justice, which would include Jewish withdrawal from all occupied territories and the establishment of a Palestinian State.

The Via Dolorosa and the Promised Land

As we examine which side God is on, whether in Palestine-Israel, Guatemala, Tibet, Afghanistan or among countless peoples caught in oppression, we are faced with the choice of how we are to respond to injustice and violence. We might be like G.K. Chesterton, who was caught in the middle of two voices during his pilgrimage to the Holy Land. On the one hand, we might see Christ accompanying the innocent oppressed along their daily walk down the Via Dolorosa. We might embrace their cries for justice against State terrorism and brutality, seeing in these helpless and desperate peoples Christ's resistance to the political injustice and religious abuse of his day — the Status Quo that, fundamentally, is out for its own profit. We might look compassionately upon those who, out of increasing and endless frustration, are forced to respond to military occupation with whatever means are available. On the other hand, we might lean toward those seeking to maintain order against terrorists who call for "holy wars" and who encourage their children to become weapons of destruction and death as suicide bombers. We might cringe at so-called "martyrs of Jerusalem," for who can win the crown of Paradise by murdering innocent people? What a far cry from the innocent, nonviolent response of the first Christian martyrs of Jerusalem, and especially the response of Jesus to his unjust treatment and execution.

Yet perhaps being caught in the tension of these opposing pulls is just the place to be if we want to walk the Way of the Cross. After all, none of us is truly innocent; our thoughts, beliefs, actions or failure to act all contribute to the environment of injustice that pervades the Holy City and surrounds us as global pilgrims. Moreover, this awareness forces us to follow all the more closely the Innocent One who walked the way of Calvary. It also forces us as peace-loving people to earnestly pray and work to achieve Archbishop Tutu's third option, so that the peace and justice of God can come to this tiny parcel of land made holy by prophets, saviors and saints. In both of these awarenesses we truly walk the narrow middle way, the Pilgrimage Way of the Cross, toward Calvary, perhaps the only holy ground that offers a possibility of real reconciliation in the Holy Land and within ourselves. As Murray Rogers said at the opening of this book, "The challenge to us Christians today is whether through our faith and life in the Resurrected Christ we will be able to transform the powers of hatred, destruction and death into a potential of love and peace."

> For the peace of Jerusalem pray:
> "May peace reign within your walls,
> in your palaces, peace!"
> For love of my family and friends,
> I say, "Peace upon you!"
> For love of the house of God,
> I pray for your good.
>   —Psalm 122: 6-9

THE AUTHOR

From a very early age Edward Hays was fascinated with travel, and before he had entered kindergarten he had twice run away from home. These preschool expeditions, while confined to very short distances, gave an early indication of a gypsy appetite to go exploring. His mother often humorously remarked that as a baby his first words were "Bye-bye" and that he has been saying them ever since.

This pilgrimage book that escorts the reader through Jerusalem had its genesis in the months the author spent in Palestine-Israel in 1971 on his way to India during an around-the-world pilgrimage. He has promised his publisher that someday before he dies he will release his personal journal of this pilgrimage to the Near and Far East. This completed book of his pilgrimage travels will have to wait its turn, however, for he is presently working on several other manuscripts.

The Author's Page that you are presently reading is usually what readers reference to find out if someone has the necessary credentials to write a book. The historical facts usually include an author's educational background and degrees, along with a list of scholastic achievements. While the author agreed to provide such credentials that have led to or marked his over forty years as a priest and over twenty-five years as a published author, he did so conditionally. Pointing out that credentials — from the Medieval Latin *credentialis*, "giving authority" — originally were letters attesting to one's authority and qualifications, he playfully suggested that a few items of his personal *creed* might be more interesting than his past scholastic or ministerial achievements in indicating his credibility as an author.

A Few *Creed*entials of Edward Hays

I believe that love is the most powerful force known in this world.
I believe that without hope the world is a corpse waiting to be
    buried.

I believe God is enfleshed in all of creation and all of the cosmos.

I believe Jesus of Galilee was a spiritual genius who more fully than anyone before or after lived out the God enfleshed in him.

I believe that God has never stopped speaking to us earthen folk — and continues to do so daily in the media, books, movies and works of art.

I believe that God uses each one of us as messengers — so we must pay attention to those we love, know and even just meet on the street.

I believe that the Divine Mystery, for some inexplicable reason, desired that this book be written.

AUTHOR'S ACKNOWLEDGMENTS

How fortunate for the author of a book on a pilgrimage to Jerusalem to have both an editor and a publisher who have made similar pilgrimages to the Holy City. I am grateful to Thomas Skorupa for his attentive editing of this manuscript and for his affirming personal recollections about the various holy sites mentioned in this book. Poring over the text with him and my publisher, Thomas Turkle, we were able to enhance the experience of the original manuscript for the reader. I thank both of these good friends and fellow pilgrims whose fingerprints can be found upon all my other books for their enormous personal investment in the process of having this pilgrimage book published.

I also acknowledge my debt of gratitude for the labor of my unnamed proofreaders and the craftsmanship of my printer, Steve Hall, and his cooperative crew of artisans at Hall Commercial Printing.